PhoneGap and AngularJS for Cross-platform Development

Build exciting cross-platform applications using PhoneGap and AngularJS

Yuxian, Eugene Liang

[PACKT] open source*
PUBLISHING   community experience distilled

BIRMINGHAM - MUMBAI

PhoneGap and AngularJS for Cross-platform Development

First published: October 2014

Production reference: 1241014

Published by Packt Publishing Ltd.
Livery Place
35 Livery Street
Birmingham B3 2PB, UK.

ISBN 978-1-78398-892-1

www.packtpub.com

Cover image by Aniket Sawant (aniket_sawant_photography@hotmail.com)

Credits

Author
Yuxian, Eugene Liang

Reviewers
Simon Basset

Razi Mahmood

Commissioning Editor
Kunal Parikh

Acquisition Editor
Meeta Rajani

Content Development Editor
Priyanka Shah

Technical Editors
Veronica Fernandes

Anand Singh

Copy Editors
Roshni Banerjee

Adithi Shetty

Project Coordinator
Kartik Vedam

Proofreaders
Maria Gould

Elinor Perry-Smith

Indexers
Monica Ajmera Mehta

Tejal Soni

Production Coordinators
Kyle Albuquerque

Nilesh R. Mohite

Cover Work
Nilesh R. Mohite

About the Author

Yuxian, Eugene Liang is a frontend engineer with working knowledge of UX and data mining / machine learning. He builds applications predominantly using JavaScript/Python, and related frameworks such as AngularJS, ReactJS, Node.js, Tornado, and Django. He led a team of two (including himself) to win Startup Weekend at Taiwan recently. He has also completed academic research on social network analysis (link prediction) using machine learning techniques, while interning as a frontend engineer at Yahoo!. To know more about him, visit `http://www.liangeugene.com`.

I am grateful for this opportunity and I want to thank the following people at Packt Publishing: Priyanka Shah, Kartik Vedam, Sageer Parkar, Meeta Rajani, and Anand Singh.

Special thanks to Professor Daphne Yuan, Professor Tsai-Yen Li, and Professor Pailin Chen of the National Cheng Chi University, Taipei, Taiwan, for providing me with timely and practical advice on how to carry out great research and how to deal with life.

To the good people of Service Science Research Center, Intelligent Media Lab, and the research team of the Flood and Fire research project, thank you for helping me out when I needed it the most.

I also want to thank XJL for helping me out and staying put when I most needed support.

Last but not least, I want to thank my family members and friends for their continued support.

About the Reviewers

Simon Basset is a cross-platform mobile and frontend engineer living in Paris. He works hard every day to create attractive mobile and web apps.

He worked for years at Smile Open Source Solutions, technically leading a team specializing in mobile development, and has recently joined the frontend expert team of AXA France.

He is a technology enthusiast. He likes to try and use cutting-edge technologies and loves the Web and open source. He also loves animals, has two cats, and is a vegetarian.

Razi Mahmood has a Master's degree in IT with 14 years of working experience, and is an accomplished and experienced software training consultant. His interest in technology never fades and he always keeps himself updated with the latest technology. As a result, he has succeeded in many areas in his career. He is motivated and is a quick learner, and has the ability to handle projects with minimum supervision; these are his personal strengths in every achievement.

Razi started his career as an executive in an engineering firm in Kuala Lumpur. Over the years, he has developed custom software solutions to expedite work in accounting, human resources, and project management reporting. These solutions were eventually documented and presented as part of his project thesis for his Master's degree. Upon completion of his Master's degree, he joined the School Of Technology Management, Binary University as a lecturer in Software Engineering and Accounting Information System. Since then, he has supervised various application development projects undertaken by students using various platforms such as Windows, Linux, OS X, Android, and iOS. In 2008, he was appointed as a member of the Panel of Assessors of Malaysian Quality Assurance Programme, specializing in databases. He is also a co-developer for an education-based mobile apps project endorsed by the Malaysian Ministry Of Education to help students learn local history subjects. This app is now featured on Google's Play store (`https://play.google.com/store/apps/details?id=com.fiziazezan2gmail.com.ism2&hl=en`).

www.PacktPub.com

Support files, eBooks, discount offers, and more

You might want to visit www.PacktPub.com for support files and downloads related to your book.

Did you know that Packt offers eBook versions of every book published, with PDF and ePub files available? You can upgrade to the eBook version at www.PacktPub.com and as a print book customer, you are entitled to a discount on the eBook copy. Get in touch with us at service@packtpub.com for more details.

At www.PacktPub.com, you can also read a collection of free technical articles, sign up for a range of free newsletters and receive exclusive discounts and offers on Packt books and eBooks.

http://PacktLib.PacktPub.com

Do you need instant solutions to your IT questions? PacktLib is Packt's online digital book library. Here, you can access, read and search across Packt's entire library of books.

Why subscribe?

- Fully searchable across every book published by Packt
- Copy and paste, print and bookmark content
- On demand and accessible via web browser

Free access for Packt account holders

If you have an account with Packt at www.PacktPub.com, you can use this to access PacktLib today and view nine entirely free books. Simply use your login credentials for immediate access.

Table of Contents

Preface

Welcome to AngularJS with PhoneGap! In this book, you will receive practical knowledge about AngularJS and PhoneGap. In particular, you will learn how to build a complete, workable web app using AngularJS, after which you will convert various versions of this web app to a PhoneGap app. You should also pick up something new regarding PhoneGap in particular: how to use the command-line interface to generate PhoneGap apps.

What this book covers

Chapter 1, Introduction to AngularJS, will teach you the absolute basics of building an AngularJS app.

Chapter 2, Getting Ready for PhoneGap, will cover the PhoneGap command-line interface. By end of this chapter, you will have learned that the command-line interface is one of the best things about PhoneGap 3.x. The example you coded in *Chapter 1, Introduction to AngularJS*, will be put to use in this chapter.

Chapter 3, From a Simple To-do List to an Advanced To-do List, will cover some of the slightly more advanced concepts of AngularJS, such as code organization, making RESTful calls, and more. This advanced app will then be converted to a PhoneGap app.

Chapter 4, Adding Authentication Capabilities Using PhoneGap Plugins, will add Facebook authentication capabilities via PhoneGap plugins. Once again, you will see how we can add the Facebook plugin using the command-line interface.

Chapter 5, Sprucing Up the App Using Animations and Mobile Design, will cover a slightly more advanced AngularJS topic: animations.

Chapter 6, Getting Ready to Launch, will teach you how to launch the app, both in Android and iOS devices.

Appendix, References, has a list of references that you should find useful.

What you need for this book

This book assumes that you have a basic code editor. You will need a Mac if you intend to develop iOS versions of the PhoneGap app. You will most definitely require an Internet connection and the Google Chrome browser.

Who this book is for

This book is intended for people who are not familiar with AngularJS but have beginner experience in PhoneGap, and who might want to improve their PhoneGap skills by learning the command-line interface for PhoneGap 3.x, and develop PhoneGap apps using AngularJS.

Conventions

In this book, you will find a number of styles of text that distinguish between different kinds of information. Here are some examples of these styles, and an explanation of their meaning.

Code words in text, database table names, folder names, filenames, file extensions, pathnames, dummy URLs, user input, and Twitter handles are shown as follows: "Feel free to copy the code and save it as `concepts.html`."

A block of code is set as follows:

```
project/
   css/
   js/
      controllers/
            todo.js
      services/
            todo.js
      app.js
   partials/
      detail.html
      list.html
   index.html
```

When we wish to draw your attention to a particular part of a code block, the relevant lines or items are set in bold:

```
<li ng-repeat="todo in todos">
  <input type="checkbox" ng-model="todo.done">
  <span class="done-{{todo.done}}">{{todo.text}}</span>
  <button ng-click="showDetail(todo.text)">Detail</button>
</li>
```

Any command-line input or output is written as follows:

```
cordova emulate android
```

New terms and **important words** are shown in bold. Words that you see on the screen, in menus or dialog boxes for example, appear in the text like this: "Click on **Edit/Details** for the Android item and start editing."

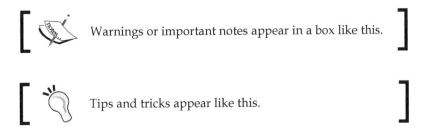

> Warnings or important notes appear in a box like this.

> Tips and tricks appear like this.

Reader feedback

Feedback from our readers is always welcome. Let us know what you think about this book—what you liked or may have disliked. Reader feedback is important for us to develop titles that you really get the most out of.

To send us general feedback, simply send an e-mail to feedback@packtpub.com, and mention the book title via the subject of your message.

If there is a topic that you have expertise in and you are interested in either writing or contributing to a book, see our author guide on www.packtpub.com/authors.

Customer support

Now that you are the proud owner of a Packt book, we have a number of things to help you to get the most from your purchase.

Downloading the example code

You can download the example code files for all Packt books you have purchased from your account at http://www.packtpub.com. If you purchased this book elsewhere, you can visit http://www.packtpub.com/support and register to have the files e-mailed directly to you.

Errata

Although we have taken every care to ensure the accuracy of our content, mistakes do happen. If you find a mistake in one of our books — maybe a mistake in the text or the code — we would be grateful if you would report this to us. By doing so, you can save other readers from frustration and help us improve subsequent versions of this book. If you find any errata, please report them by visiting http://www.packtpub.com/submit-errata, selecting your book, clicking on the **errata submission form** link, and entering the details of your errata. Once your errata are verified, your submission will be accepted and the errata will be uploaded on our website, or added to any list of existing errata, under the Errata section of that title. Any existing errata can be viewed by selecting your title from http://www.packtpub.com/support.

Piracy

Piracy of copyright material on the Internet is an ongoing problem across all media. At Packt, we take the protection of our copyright and licenses very seriously. If you come across any illegal copies of our works, in any form, on the Internet, please provide us with the location address or website name immediately so that we can pursue a remedy.

Please contact us at copyright@packtpub.com with a link to the suspected pirated material.

We appreciate your help in protecting our authors, and our ability to bring you valuable content.

Questions

You can contact us at questions@packtpub.com if you are having a problem with any aspect of the book, and we will do our best to address it.

1
Introduction to AngularJS

Welcome to the world of AngularJS with PhoneGap! In this book, you will learn how to merge two very exciting technologies, namely AngularJS and PhoneGap. By the end of this book, you will have a working mobile app that works across iOS and Android, based on AngularJS and PhoneGap. As mentioned previously, this book is targeted at programmers who have knowledge of PhoneGap, but may or may not have knowledge regarding AngularJS. You should have some idea about JavaScript though, for you to get maximum benefit out of this book. That said, let us begin with AngularJS.

A brief overview of AngularJS

AngularJS (https://angularjs.org/) is a super heroic JavaScript MVC framework, which is maintained by Google. It is open source and its main goal is to assist with creating single page applications. These are typically one-page web applications that only require HTML, CSS, and JavaScript on the client side.

While one may argue that there are already many frameworks out there in the market that help with this issue, I would like to say that AngularJS is different in a few ways. And in quite a few of these instances, it makes your life much easier as a frontend programmer.

Core concepts

There are many concepts related to AngularJS, but I will cover the most commonly used ones for the sake of progressing through this chapter. As we go along in this book, I'll touch on other concepts, such as the use of self-defined directives and performing RESTful requests via AngularJS. The main concepts that you should understand in this section are directives, controllers, and data binding.

Controllers

If you have already used JavaScript frameworks, such as BackBone.js, Can.js, Ember.js, or KnockOut.js, you should be familiar with this concept. Controllers are the behavior behind the DOM elements. AngularJS lets you express the behavior in a clean readable form without the usual boilerplate of updating the DOM, registering callbacks, or watching model changes.

Data-binding

Data-binding is an automatic way to update the view whenever the model changes, as well as updating the model whenever the view changes. The coolest aspect of this concept is that it is a two way data-binding process. Used in tandem with controllers, this can save you a lot of code, as there is no need for you to write the usual updating of the DOM elements.

Directives

Directives are another awesome concept in AngularJS. What they do is teach your application new HTML syntax and new things specific to your application. Directives can be self-defined and predefined. Some of the more notable predefined directives include:

- ng-app: This declares an element as a root element of the application, allowing its behavior to be modified through custom HTML tags.

- ng-bind: This automatically changes the text of an HTML element to the value of a given expression.

- ng-model: This is similar to ng-bind, but allows two-way binding between the view and scope.

- ng-controller: This specifies a JavaScript controller class, which evaluates HTML expressions. In layman's terms, what ng-controller does is that it applies a JavaScript function to this block of HTML so that this particular JavaScript function (including its accompanying logic, expressions, and more) can only operate in this block of HTML.

- ng-repeat: You can see this as a loop through a collection.

A conceptual example

Now, let's take a look at how some of the previous concepts play together.
Consider the following piece of code:

```html
<!doctype html>
<html ng-app>
  <head>
    <script src="https://ajax.googleapis.com/ajax/libs/
angularjs/1.2.12/angular.min.js"></script>
  </head>
  <body>
    <div>
      <label>Say Hello World</label>
      <input type="text" ng-model="yourHelloWorld" placeholder="Type
anything here.">
      <hr>
      <h1>Hello {{yourHelloWorld}}!</h1>
    </div>
  </body>
</html>
```

Let's go through the code.

- We defined an HTML5 HTML document in this case, as seen in the first line
- Next, notice ng-app in the second line of the code; this is an
  AngularJS directive, which tells AngularJS that this is the root of the
  AngularJS application
- In order to use AngularJS, we obviously have to install the script on
  this web page, as shown in the <script> tag
- Within the body tag, we see a label, an input, and an h1 tag.
- Take note of the input tag, there is a ng-model directive, which is mapped
  to h1 tag's {{yourHelloWorld}}
- What the previous piece of code does is that anything that is typed into
  the input box, will be shown in place of {{yourHelloWorld}}

Take note of the version of the code we are using in this chapter, version 1.2.12;
should you be using newer versions of AngularJS, there is no guarantee that the
code will work.

Now that we have briefly walked through the code, let us copy the code and run it on our web browser. Feel free to copy the code and save it as concepts.html. The source code for this chapter can be found in the concepts.html file in the Chapter 1 folder.

Copied the code? If so, open the file in your favorite web browser. You should see the following screenshot in your browser:

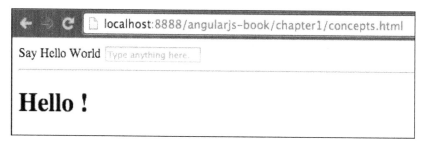

A sample concept web page

Got the previous code? Ok great! So now you can try typing into the input box and see new text being appended to **Hello** and before **!** in the screen.

For instance, when we type world, we will see the new characters being appended to the screen as I continue to type. By the end of typing the word "World", we should see the following screenshot:

After typing World

Now that we have a brief idea as to how a simple AngularJS app works, let us move to a more complicated app.

A simple to-do list using AngularJS

In this example, we will cover in detail as to how to write code for a slightly more complicated AngularJS app. This app is modified from the official example found at angularjs.org. This example will be used as a base when we convert it from a web application to a PhoneGap application.

Preparing your code structure

For starters, create the `index.html` and `todo.js` files. Just for your information, the code found in this section can be found in the `todo` folder in `Chapter 1`.

HTML for our to-do list

We need to prepare our HTML file so that we can make use of AngularJS. Similar to the previous `concepts.html` file, you will see that we have included the use of AngularJS via script. Open up your `index.html` file in your favorite editor and you can start by adding the following code:

```html
<!doctype html>
<html ng-app>
  <head>
    <script src="https://ajax.googleapis.com/ajax/libs/
angularjs/1.2.12/angular.min.js"></script>
    <script src="todo.js"></script>
    <link rel="stylesheet" href="http://netdna.bootstrapcdn.com/
bootstrap/3.0.3/css/bootstrap.min.css">
    <style>
      body {
        padding:40px;
      }
      #todoDetails {
        visibility: hidden;
      }
    </style>
  </head>
  <body>
    <div class="row"  ng-controller="todoCtrl">
      <div class="col-md-6">
        <h2>Todo</h2>
        <div>
          <span>{{getRemaining()}} of {{todos.length}} remaining</span>
          [ <button ng-click="archive()">archive</button> ]
          <ul class="unstyled">
            <li ng-repeat="todo in todos">
              <input type="checkbox" ng-model="todo.done">
              <span class="done-{{todo.done}}">{{todo.text}}</span>
              <button ng-click="showDetail(todo.text)">Detail</button>
            </li>
          </ul>
          <form ng-submit="addTodo()">
```

```
        <input type="text" ng-model="todoText"   size="30"
                placeholder="add new todo here">
        <input class="btn-primary" type="submit" value="add">
      </form>
    </div>
  </div>
  <div id="todoDetails" class="col-md-6" >
    <h2>Details</h2>
    Title: <span id="title">{{currentText}}</span>
    <br>
    Add Details:
    <form ng-submit="addDetails()">
      <textarea id="details" ng-model="currentDetails">{{currentDe
tails}}</textarea>
      <p>
      <input class="btn-primary" type="submit" value="Add
Details">
      <input class="btn-primary" type="submit" value="Cancel" ng-
click="closeThis()">
      </p>
    </form>
  </div>
    </div>
  </body>
</html>
```

Now, to make sure that you are on the same page as I am, I want you to open this file in your favorite browser. You should see something like the following screenshot:

Our HTML template

Got the previous code? It looks weird now due to the fact that we have not added the main JavaScript functionalities. We will be working on it in the next section.

Now, let me explain the code; notice that I have highlighted a few lines of it. These are the most important lines of the code that you should take note of in this example. The remaining lines are just the usual HTML code.

- The first two lines of the highlighted code simply install AngularJS and include BootStrap 3's CSS for styling purposes. Without both, the project will not work and may not look good.

- The `ng-controller` directive is what we covered briefly earlier on in this chapter. We are applying `todoCtrl` to this block of HTML.

- The `ng-click` directive is another directive that we did not touch on in the previous section. What `ng-click` does is that it executes whatever function is defined for this directive. In our example, `ng-click="archive()"` means that on clicking it, `archive()` will be executed. The JavaScript function `archive()` is written in our `todo.js` file, which we will cover later.

- The `ng-repeat` directive is a directive that loops through a collection. Notice how we implemented `ng-repeat` in our HTML code:

  ```
  <li ng-repeat="todo in todos">
      <input type="checkbox" ng-model="todo.done">
      <span class="done-{{todo.done}}">{{todo.text}}</span>
      <button ng-click="showDetail(todo.text)">Detail</button>
  </li>
  ```

  Anything that is within `<li>` is dependent on the `todo` object, which is part of the `todos` collection.

- The `ng-submit` directive is generally used in forms. This is a directive which controls what is being done on the submit form. In this case, on the submit form, we will execute the JavaScript function `addToDo()`.

- The `[]` option encapsulates `<button ng-click="archive()">archive</button>`, which simply adds a square bracket around the button.

Adding in JavaScript with AngularJS

Now we will open our `todo.js` file, which we created in the previous section. Open `todo.js` in your favorite text editor. Let us begin by coding the following:

```
function todoCtrl($scope) {

}
```

We are first going to define a controller, which we will be using for our app. Notice that we have named it `todoCtrl`, which is mapped onto `ng-controller` in the HTML file (`index.html`), where `ng-controller="todoCtrl"` means that `todoCtrl` will be controlling this portion of the web page.

Also, notice the use of `$scope`, which is an object that refers to the application model; it is the execution context for related expressions, such as `ng-click`, `ng-model`, and so on. Any such expressions of a predefined directive outside this scope will not be executed.

Let's start by initializing our to-do list. Within `todoCtrl`, add the following code:

```
$scope.todos = [
    {text:'here is my first to do', done:true, details:''},
    {text:'continue writing chapter 1 for this book', done:false,
details:''},
    {text:'work on chapter 2 examples', done:false, details:''}
];

$scope.currentText = ''; // make the text empty
$scope.currentDetails = ''; // make the text empty
```

What `$scope.todos` does is that it simply creates a list of objects, which contains the text, details, and whether this to-do is executed or not (true or false). Notice that `todos` here is mapped to the collection `todos` as seen in `index.html`, where `ng-repeat` is being used.

Let's move on by adding more functionalities. After `$scope.currentDetails`, add the following three JavaScript functions:

```
$scope.addTodo = function() {
    $scope.todos.push({text:$scope.todoText, done:false, details:''});
    $scope.todoText = '';
};

$scope.remaining = function() {
    var count = 0;
    angular.forEach($scope.todos, function(todo) {
        count += todo.done ? 0 : 1;
    });
    return count;
};

$scope.archive = function() {
    var oldTodos = $scope.todos;
    $scope.todos = [];
```

```
    angular.forEach(oldTodos, function(todo) {
      if (!todo.done) $scope.todos.push(todo);
    });
  };
```

The `$scope.todoText` function resets `todoText` after it has been pushed into the array. The `$scope.addTodo` function does what it is suppose to do, simply adding a new to-do to the list of `todos` as defined earlier. The beauty of AngularJS is that it uses standard JavaScript data structures that make manipulation so much easier.

The `$scope.getRemaining` function simply calculates the number of items that are not done yet. Here, we can see two-way data-binding in action as this function executes whenever there is a change in the length of `todos`.

The `$scope.archive` function marks a to-do as `done:true` in standard JavaScript manner.

By now, you should have noticed that all the JavaScript functions defined here are being used in `index.html` under `ng-controller="todoCtrl"`.

Let's now add three more JavaScript functions to complete the finishing touch for this sample application.

After the `$scope.archive` function, add the following functions:

```
    $scope.showDetail = function(text) {
      var result = $scope.todos.filter(function (obj) {
        return obj.text == text;
      })
      $scope.currentText = result[0].text;
      $scope.currentDetails = result[0].details;
      document.getElementById('todoDetails').style.visibility =
  'visible';
    }

  $scope.closeThis = function() {
    $scope.currentText = '';
    $scope.currentDetails = '';
    document.getElementById('todoDetails').style.visibility =
  'hidden';
    }

  $scope.addDetails = function(text) {
    var result = $scope.todos.filter(function (obj) {
      return obj.text == text;
    })
```

```
angular.forEach($scope.todos, function(todo) {
    if(todo.text == text) {
        todo.details = $scope.currentDetails;
    }
});
document.getElementById('todoDetails').style.visibility =
'hidden';


}
```

The $scope.showDetail function simply retrieves the current to-do being clicked on and shows it on the div with ID #todoDetails. The visibility of the #todoDetails function is then set to visible.

The $scope.close function simply changes the visibility of #todoDetails to hidden.

Finally, $scope.addDetails adds the details of the todo item, and changes the visibility of #todoDetails to hidden once done.

Okay, so to see if we are on the same page, we now need to check our code. Save this file as todo.js. Refresh your browser and you should still see the same user interface as per the previous screenshot.

Now, try clicking on the **Detail** button in front of **work on chapter 2 examples**, and you should see the following screenshot:

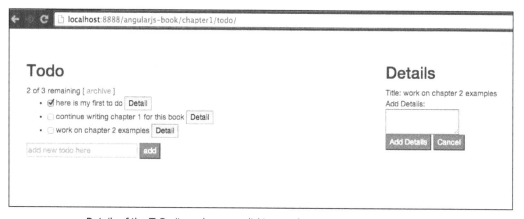

Details of the ToDo item shows on clicking on the corresponding detail button

You will see the details of a particular to-do item. You can try to add some details for this item and click on **Add Details**. You can then click on other items and come back to this item later (without refreshing the browser), and you should still see the details in the text area.

You can also check off any of the items and you will see that the number of remaining to-do item decreases:

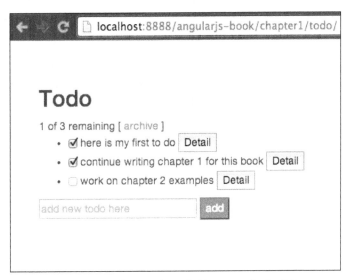

Number of items changes dynamically as you check off items

And of course, you can add new items by simply typing in the input box and clicking on the **add** button. You should notice that the number of items now increases:

Adding new to-dos changes the number of items dynamically and also shows on the screen immediately

Summary

To summarize what we have done in this chapter; we have walked through the basics of building an AngularJS app and familiarized ourselves with the basic concepts used in AngularJS. We have made use of ng-app, ng-controller, ng-click, ng-repeat, and ng-submit in general. These expressions, such as ng-click and ng-submit are typically mapped onto JavaScript functions defined in AngularJS controllers, as seen in todo.js in our example. Notice how little code we have written in order to achieve such speedy UX through the concept of two-way data-binding and its controllers.

In the next chapter, we will start to port this app in a more organized manner to PhoneGap.

Getting Ready for PhoneGap

2

As you might already know, PhoneGap (http://phonegap.com/) is a really cool open source project (now owned by Adobe), that allows you to create cross platform mobile apps using JavaScript/CSS/HTML.

This means that you can readily use your web development skills to developing mobile apps. Since this book assumes basic familiarity with PhoneGap, I will advance to how to install PhoneGap. You will primarily see examples related to Android and iOS since we are going to create mobiles apps that only support Android and iOS.

Note that we are focusing on using PhoneGap Version 3.3.0 and, as much as possible, we will be building the apps via the latest command-line interface provided by PhoneGap.

Just for your information, all source code found in this chapter—whether automatically generated by PhoneGap or coded by us—can be found in the source code folder, chapter2.

Preparing for PhoneGap development

We will now go quickly through the installation process for Android and iOS platforms. The basic instructions for this section can be found at http://docs. phonegap.com/en/3.3.0/guide_platforms_index.md.html#Platform%20Guides.

Installing Android

The instructions to install Android SDK can be found at `http://docs.phonegap.com/en/3.3.0/guide_platforms_android_index.md.html#Android%20Platform%20Guide`.

In order to benefit from this chapter, you need to follow the instructions till the point where you can run the Hello World example in your Android emulator. This will include things like installing the Android SDK, Eclipse Tools, and so on.

Installing iOS

If you are using Mac and want to develop an app for iOS, then you will need to install the SDK for iOS as well. In general, you will need to install Xcode from the App Store and you will need to register as an Apple Developer in order to deploy the app in the App Store.

You can follow the instructions given at `http://docs.phonegap.com/en/3.3.0/guide_platforms_ios_index.md.html#iOS%20Platform%20Guide`.

Please make sure that you can at least run the PhoneGap Hello World example in your iOS simulator in order to benefit from this chapter.

Command-line interface for both Android and iOS

Once you have finished installing the individual platforms, it's time to move on to the command-line interface. This section contains the most important commands for the command-line interface. To start off, you need to install Node.js (`www.nodejs.org`). Once you have installed `node.js`, perform the following steps:

1. Run the `npm -g install cordova` command. This installs the command-line interface on your computer.

2. Change the directory to the place where you will be saving your project files for this chapter.

3. Once in the directory, issue the `cordova create todo com.project.todo ToDo` command. This will create a folder containing your basic files for PhoneGap.

4. Now, change directory to `/todo`.

5. Once in the directory, we need to install the various platforms we will be supporting:

   ° For iOS, use the `cordova platform add ios` command

   ° For Android, use the `cordova platform add android` command

6. Now, let's try to run the Hello World example in Android using the `cordova emulate android` command. If you see an area where you have not defined an AVD, run the `android create avd -name todo -target 1` command.

7. Then, run the `cordova emulate android` again command. If everything works correctly, you should see the following screenshot:

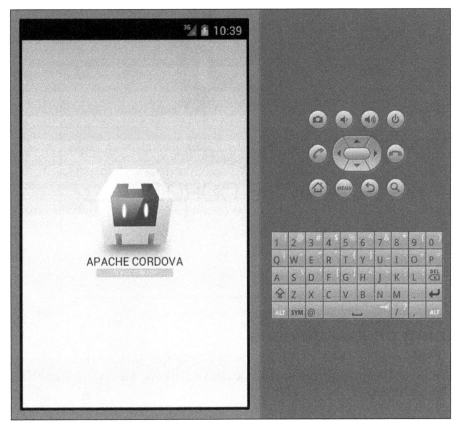

Hello World working in android

Cool, so now let's try to run the Hello World example in an iOS simulator. For a start, issue the `node -g install ios-sim` command. Now, run the `cordova emulate ios` command. If everything runs correctly, you should see the following screenshot:

Running on real devices

So far, we have learned how to run the Hello World app on emulators. However, what if we want to run our code on our devices ? It's easy; for android, run the following commands:

```
cordova build android
cordova run android
```

For iOS, run the following commands:

```
cordova build ios
cordova run ios
```

Got the previous example running? If so, great! Let's now move on to the next section where we implement AngularJS on PhoneGap.

AngularJS on PhoneGap

Before we begin this section, let's take a look at how much *magic* the PhoneGap command-line interface has. Navigate to the directory where you saved your code; you should see something like the following screenshot:

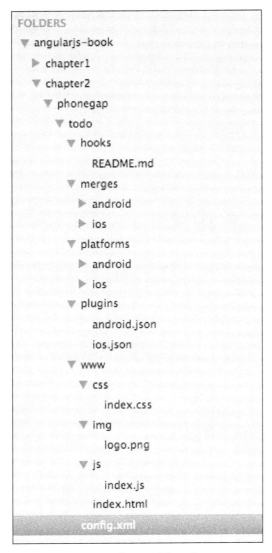

Directory layout of the code

The previous screenshot is how my code directory looks after issuing the PhoneGap commands of the previous section. Notice that I've created the folder phonegap/, and the PhoneGap command line helped us create the todo/ project folder with other folders such as hooks/, merges/, platforms/, plugins/, and so on. Our platform-specific commands created the folders android/ and ios/ and they are found under merges/ and platforms/ respectively.

The automatically created folders are meant to hold important files that belong to different platforms. For example, you will find Android-related files in android, while you will find iOS related files in ios/. In the plugins/ folder, you will find the various plugins that you have installed. Later in this book, you will see and experience the Facebook connect plugin.

In my opinion, the command-line interface saves us a lot of work. Most importantly, we are not tied down to any particular code editor; we can just use the terminal and any code editor that we prefer (I use Sublime Text).

Now, going back to your source code, navigate to the www/ folder under todo/. As you might already know, www/ contains our source code for the JavaScript, CSS, and HTML files.

Look for the index.html file and rename it index_backup.html. Now, create a new index.html file under the www/ directory.

Next, copy and paste the contents from concepts.html, but make a few changes to it. For your convenience, the code that we will use is as follows:

```html
<!doctype html>
<html ng-app>
  <head>
    <script type="text/javascript" src="cordova.js"></script>
    <script src="https://ajax.googleapis.com/ajax/libs/
angularjs/1.2.12/angular.min.js"></script>
    <style>
        body {
            padding:40px;
        }
        #holder {
            border: 2px solid red;
        }
    </style>
  </head>
<body>
  <div id="holder">
    <label>Say Hello World</label>
```

```
    <input type="text" ng-model="yourHelloWorld" placeholder="Type
anything here.">
    <hr>
    <h1>Hello {{yourHelloWorld}}!</h1>
  </div>
  </body>
</html>
```

The code is generally the same as the `concepts.html` file as seen in the `chapter1` folder, but with a few changes as shown in the highlighted lines of code:

- In the `<header>` tag, we installed PhoneGap by using `<script type="text/javascript" src="cordova.js">`
- Next, we added simple styles so that we can see what we are concerned with bounded in a red box

Now, save your code as `index.html`. Make sure it is saved under the www/ folder. After you have saved it, we need to test the code and make sure that the code is working as per what we have seen in the `chapter1` folder. We should expect to see that as we type any text into the input box, it should be appended after the **Hello!** text.

So now, let's start testing our code. Let's start with iOS. Go to your terminal and make sure you change the directory to `todo/`. Once in the directory, issue the command `cordova emulate ios`. Once your emulator has started, you should see the following screenshot:

AngularJS Hello World example on PhoneGap iOS Simulator

All is good. Now let's test by typing into the text input and see if it works as intended. In my case, I typed, hey, and I got the following screenshot:

Typing hey to make sure that the code works

Understood the example? Make sure that the characters get printed out as you type along! If iOS is working out fine, we should not have any problem with Android. However, for safety's sake, let's fire up Android's emulator to make sure things are going as intended.

Quit your iOS simulator if you want to. Now, return to your terminal and issue the command cordova emulate android. Once Android's emulator has started, you should see the following screenshot:

AngularJS Hello World on Android emulator

If you got the output, that's good. Let's test by typing into the text input box. This time, I typed `world` and I got the following screenshot:

AngularJS Hello World on iOS simulator

What just happened?

By now, you should have noticed that enabling AngularJS on PhoneGap apps are pretty straightforward, just code as if you are writing an AngularJS app. To port it over to PhoneGap, just make sure you run the commands shown in the previous sections and install the `cordova.js` script in your AngularJS app.

Now that we have made sure that AngularJS works in PhoneGap, it's time to move on to the main topic of this chapter: building a Todo app.

Creating a to-do list app using AngularJS on PhoneGap

For this section, we'll start off by transferring the to-do list app from the `chapter1` folder to PhoneGap. As you may have already guessed, shifting the to-do list app to a PhoneGap version simply requires the installation of `cordova.js`. Let's see how this is done in the next section.

A basic version of a to-do list using AngularJS on PhoneGap

Let's quickly get started by shifting the to-do list app from `chapter1` to PhoneGap. Perform the following steps:

1. Change the directory to `chapter2` and navigate to `www/` where your PhoneGap files are located.

2. Change `index.html` to `index_concepts.html`.

3. Now, copy the contents from `index.html` from `chapter1` (where the basic HTML structure for todo app resides) to our new `index.html` file.

4. Copy `todo.js` from `todo/` in `chapter1` to `js/` in `www/` in the `chapter2` folder.

Your directory should look like this for **todo** app of **chapter2**:

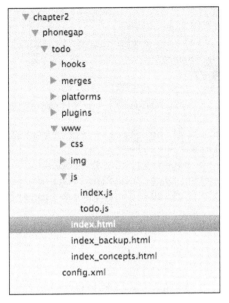

The code directory

5. So, as of now, your `index.html` file for this chapter should look like the following code:

```
<!doctype html>
<html ng-app>
  <head>
    <script src="https://ajax.googleapis.com/ajax/libs/
angularjs/1.2.12/angular.min.js"></script>
    <script src="todo.js"></script>
    <link rel="stylesheet" href="http://netdna.bootstrapcdn.com/
bootstrap/3.0.3/css/bootstrap.min.css">
    <style>
      body {
        padding:40px;
      }
      #todoDetails {
        visibility: hidden;
```

```html
          }
        </style>
    </head>
    <body>
      <div class="row"  ng-controller="todoCtrl">
        <div class="col-md-6">
          <h2>Todo</h2>
          <div>
            <span>{{remaining()}} of {{todos.length}} remaining</span>
            [ <a href="" ng-click="archive()">archive</a> ]
            <ul class="unstyled">
              <li ng-repeat="todo in todos">
                <input type="checkbox" ng-model="todo.done">
                <span class="done-{{todo.done}}">{{todo.text}}</span>
                <button ng-click="showDetail(todo.text)">Detail</button>
              </li>
            </ul>
            <form ng-submit="addTodo()">
              <input type="text" ng-model="todoText"  size="30"
                     placeholder="add new todo here">
              <input class="btn-primary" type="submit" value="add">
            </form>
          </div>
        </div>
        <div id="todoDetails" class="col-md-6" >
          <h2>Details</h2>
          Title: <span id="title">{{currentText}}</span>
          <br>
          Add Details:
          <form ng-submit="addDetails(currentText)">
            <textarea id="details" ng-model="currentDetails">{{currentDetails}}</textarea>
            <p>
            <input class="btn-primary" type="submit" value="Add Details">
            <input class="btn-primary" type="submit" value="Cancel" ng-click="closeThis()">
            </p>
          </form>
        </div>
      </div>
    </body>
</html>
```

Let's make some CSS changes to the code that you are going to use for `index.html`; we need to change the highlighted line of code to `padding:40px 20px 0 20px;`.

6. Now, we need to fire up our code to make sure that it is working as intended. We'll test it out on iOS first. Go to your terminal, change the directory to `todo/` and issue the command `cordova emulate ios`. Once the iOS simulator is fired up, you should see the following screenshot:

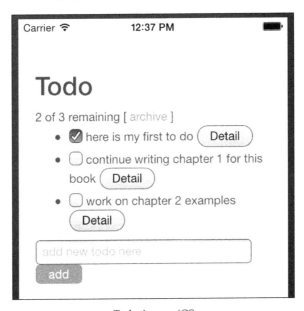

Todo App on iOS

7. Now test the following to make sure that it is working as per what we see in `chapter1`:

   ° Tick off the check boxes to see if the number of tasks remaining and total tasks are correct

   ° Try adding a new todo item and see if it adds to the list of todos

° Click on **Detail** and see if the item will show up below the input box. For instance, you should see something like the following screenshot:

Details for each todo item

If you are getting the preceding tests right, then congratulations; all is working well and good. Now we need to test the code on Android. Going back to your terminal, issue the command `cordova emulate android`. After the emulator is fired up, you should see the following:

Todo app on Android

Now, as usual, carry out the test that you have done for iOS. Similarly, when you click on the **Detail** button, you should see the following screenshot:

Todo details for each todo on Android

Summary

Let's quickly discuss what we have done in this chapter. We have prepared ourselves for PhoneGap development by installing SDKs for both Android and iOS. Next, we touched on how we can make use of PhoneGap command-line interface to set up our app, install, and prepare for different platforms and run our apps on iOS and Android emulators. We've also learned the commands to run our apps on real devices.

However, we are still far away from a decent mobile app. What we have now is just a basic version of the todo app on PhoneGap; we need to improve on it. Specifically, we need to make it look more like a mobile app. For instance, can we design the look and feel of the to-do list so that it when we tap on it, we are shown the individual todo item on a single page, instead of just appending it to the bottom of the page? We'll do this and more in the next chapter.

3
From a Simple To-do List to an Advanced To-do List

Now that we have our basics in place, let's move on to something more advanced. In *Chapter 1*, *Introduction to AngularJS*, and *Chapter 2*, *Getting Ready for PhoneGap*, we built a simple to-do list, which works well, but the code organization is amateurish at best. The code arrangement in the previous chapters prevents us from writing large apps should we want to. Hence, in this chapter, we will start off by reorganizing the code first, before wiring up with a backend server.

We will be building on the topics covered in *Chapter 1*, *Introduction to AngularJS*, and *Chapter 2*, *Getting Ready for PhoneGap*. Specifically, we are going to cover three main areas:

* Reorganizing the code
* Writing our server using the Tornado web server
* Wiring our app with the backend server

Rewriting the simple to-do list app

In *Chapter 2*, *Getting Ready for PhoneGap*, we wrote a rather simplistic version of the to-do list app. As you may have already noticed, many things were missing; there was no backend server to save your to-do lists, and there was no code organization, as everything was just written within a folder and with minimal breakup of the code.

In this section, we are going to do just that; rewrite the code so that there are some levels of code organization.

Let's review the code organization first. The app we built in *Chapter 1, Introduction to AngularJS*, looks like the following:

```
todo/
    todo.js
    index.html
```

We are going to break up the code so that the code organization looks as follows:

```
project/
    css/
    js/
        controllers/
                todo.js
        services/
                todo.js
        app.js
    partials/
        detail.html
        list.html
    index.html
```

So what is going to happen is that `project.js` from *Chapter 2, Getting Ready for PhoneGap*, will be broken up into `todo.js`, `controllers/todo.js`, `services/todo.js`, and `app.js`. We will also breakup `index.html` into multiple HTML snippets and place them under the `partials/` folder.

So before you start with the next section, you might want to create the directories and empty files based on the code organization.

Splitting index.html into multiple files

We will start work on `index.html` first. To start off, this is what `index.html` will look like in this chapter:

```html
<!doctype html>
<html ng-app="todoApp">
  <head>
    <link rel="stylesheet" href="http://netdna.bootstrapcdn.com/
      bootstrap/3.0.3/css/bootstrap.min.css">
    <style>
    body {
      padding: 40px 20px 0 20px;
    }
    </style>
```

```
<script src="https://ajax.googleapis.com/ajax/libs/
  angularjs/1.2.12/angular.min.js"></script>
<script src="https://ajax.googleapis.com/ajax/libs/
  angularjs/1.2.12/angular-resource.min.js">
</script>
<script src="https://ajax.googleapis.com/ajax/libs/
  angularjs/1.2.12/angular-route.min.js">
</script>
<script src="js/controllers/todo.js"></script>
<script src="js/services/todo.js"></script>
<script src="js/app.js"></script>
</head>
<body>
  <h2>Todos</h2>
  <div ng-view></div>
</body>
</html>
```

The preceding code structure is essentially the same as what we saw in *Chapter 2, Getting Ready for PhoneGap*. The main difference is that much of the details (such as listing the to-do lists and edit view) are now being abstracted away.

The main thing to note is the use of ng-view in index.html; you can think of ng-view as a container that will *hold* different snippets of HTML based on the current URL.

Now let's begin coding:

1. Let's work on partials/detail.html:

```
<form name="myForm">
  <div class="control-group">
    <label>Name</label>
    <input type="text" name="text" ng-model="todoText">
  </div>
  <div class="control-group">
    <label>Details</label>
    <textarea name="description"
      ng-model="todoDetails"></textarea>
  </div>
  <br>
  <a href="#/" class="btn">Cancel</a>
  <button ng-click="save()"
          class="btn btn-primary">Save</button>
  <button ng-click="destroy()"
          ng-show="project.$remove" class="btn
            btn-    danger">Delete</button>

</form>
```

2. You will see some of the details of the `detail.html` file in the previous chapter; the highlighted lines of code are the new additions:

   ° `<a href="#/" class="btn">Cancel</a>` simply performs a change in the URL route when we perform a cancel action. Notice that we are using #/ instead of /.

   ° Instead of using `ng-submit` to add new to-do lists, we now use `ng-click="save()"` to either create or edit the current to-do item, should there be any.

3. Once you're done with the preceding step, let's move to `partials/list.html`:

```html
<span>{{remaining()}} of {{todos.length}} remaining</span>
<table>
  <thead>
  <tr>
    <th>Todo</th>
    <th>Done</th>
    <th>Details</th>
    <th><a href="#/new"><i class="icon-plus-sign">NEW</i>
      </a></th>
  </tr>
  </thead>
  <tbody>
  <tr ng-repeat="todo in todos">
    <td>{{todo.text}}</td>
    <td><input type="checkbox" ng-model="todo.done"></td>
    <td>
      <a href="#/edit/{{todo.text}}"><i class="icon-
        pencil">Edit/Details</i></a>
    </td>
  </tr>
  </tbody>
</table>
```

4. The `list.html` file is similar to what we have done in *Chapter 2, Getting Ready for PhoneGap*; the only change was that we split the part where we loop through the list of to-dos into a separate HTML file.

Now that we are done with the HTML portion of the code, let's move on to the meat of this rewrite: rearranging the JavaScript code.

Splitting todo.js into multiple files

We will first work on app.js found under the project/js folder. Bear in mind that this is the first time we write the code for app.js. It contains the routes to different views of the app by making use of an AngularJS module called ngRoute.

Now let's see how we can make use of ngRoute:

1. To start off, here's what app.js looks like now:

```
angular.module('todoApp', [
  'ngRoute',
  'todoApp.controllers',
  'todoApp.services'
])

.config(function($routeProvider) {
  $routeProvider
    .when('/', {
      controller:'ListCtrl',
      templateUrl:'partials/list.html'
    })
    .when('/edit/:todoText', {
      controller:'EditCtrl',
      templateUrl:'partials/detail.html'
    })
    .when('/new', {
      controller:'CreateCtrl',
      templateUrl:'partials/detail.html'
    })
    .otherwise({
      redirectTo:'/'
    });
})
```

2. Let's go through what's happening here line by line:
   - We first define todoApp; something we have done in *Chapter 1, Introduction to AngularJS,* and *Chapter 2, Getting Ready for PhoneGap.*
   - Next, we included the modules and code that we want to use, namely ngRoute, todoApp.controller, and todoApp.services. Take note that we have not created todoApp.controller and todoApp.services yet.
   - Finally, we make use of the ngRoute module to define the routes we want to use, and its associated controller and template.

- ○ when('/' means that when the URL location is '/', we will be using ListCtrl and the partials/list.html template.
- ○ Controllers in each of the route are defined as todoApp.controllers (which is the controller.js file we will be working on in the next section).
- ○ templateurl is simply the HTML snippet that we would like to show for each different URL.

3. Now let's create the controller found at controller/todo.js. The code is the same as in *Chapter 2, Getting Ready for PhoneGap*:

```
angular.module('todoApp.controllers',[])
    .controller('ListCtrl', function($scope, $http, Todos) {
      $scope.todos = Todos;
      $scope.remaining = function() {
        var count = 0;
        angular.forEach($scope.todos, function(todo) {
          count += todo.done ? 0 : 1;
        });
        return count;
      };

    })
    .controller('CreateCtrl', function($scope, $location,
      $timeout, Todos) {
      $scope.todoText = "";
      $scope.todoDetails = ""
      $scope.save = function() {
        Todos.push({text:$scope.todoText, done:false,
          details:$scope.todoDetails});
        $location.path('/');
      };
    })
    .controller('EditCtrl',
      function($scope, $location, $routeParams, Todos) {
        $scope.todos = Todos;

        var result = $scope.todos.filter(function (obj) {
          return obj.text == $routeParams.todoText;
        });
        $scope.todoText = result[0].text;
        $scope.todoDetails = result[0].details;
        $scope.save = function() {
          var text = $scope.todoText;
```

```
              var details = $scope.todoDetails;
              var done = $scope.todoDone;
              alert(text);
              angular.forEach($scope.todos, function(todo) {
                if(todo.text == text) {
                  todo.text = text;
                  todo.details = details;
                }
              });
              $location.path('/');
            };
            $scope.destroy = function() {
              $scope.project.$remove();
              $location.path('/');
            };

          });
```

4. The only line of code you need to take note of is the first line; we have defined `todoApp.controllers`, which was referenced from `js/app.js` earlier on.

5. We can now move on to `js/services/todo.js`. As usual, we first declare `todoApp.services`, followed by `Todos`. We simply return a list of to-do items here. The code looks as follows:

```
angular.module('todoApp.services', [])
  .factory('Todos', function() {
      var items = [
        {text:'here is my first to do', done:true,
          details:''},
        {text:'continue writing chapter 1 for this book',
          done:false, details:''},
        {text:'work on chapter 2 examples', done:false,
          details:''}
      ]
      return items;
  })
```

Now that we have more or less reorganized our code, we should check that our code is working. Save your code and open up `index.html` in your web browser. You should expect to see that the code is working as per *Chapter 2, Getting Ready for PhoneGap*. The interface will look the same with the exception that the underlying code's organization has changed.

Is it all working well? If so, great! You can proceed to create a PhoneGap version of this code by copying and pasting the contents of `todos_advance/` into the `www/` folder found in your PhoneGap project.

Next, you can test your code in the Android and iOS emulators by running `cordova emulator android` and `cordova emulator ios`, respectively, and making sure that the code is working fine.

Checkpoint

Now that we have rewritten the code and transferred it to PhoneGap, check if the `www/` directory in your PhoneGap app looks like the following:

```
www/
    css/
    js/
        controllers/
            todo.js
        services/
            todo.js
    partials/
        detail.html
        list.html
    index.html
```

Most importantly, make sure that your code in PhoneGap is working as per *Chapter 2, Getting Ready for PhoneGap*. Also, your app should look and work similarly to the version we have coded we have in *Chapter 2, Getting Ready for PhoneGap*. If the code is confirmed and working correctly, let's move on to the next section where we wire a backend server and create an advanced version of the to-do list app.

Wiring up a backend server

In this section, we will make use of the `$http` module of AngularJS to make RESTful calls to a simple backend server. The backend server here is based on Facebook's Tornado Framework (`https://github.com/facebook/tornado/`), but the fact is that you can make RESTful calls using Express.js (`http://expressjs.com/`) or any other framework that you like.

Before you get started with this section, you will need to have MongoDB (`http://www.mongodb.org/`), Python 2.7.x, and the Tornado web server installed. You will also need to install a Python library called `tornado-cor` (`https://github.com/globocom/tornado-cors`), which facilitates the use of cross-origin resources between your AngularJS app and server.

Coding our server

The main idea of the Python Tornado server is as follows:

- We have one endpoint, where this endpoint will receive a GET or POST request from our AngularJS app.

- Depending on the URL argument received, the corresponding handler will perform GET on all to-do items or one to-do item. If the request is a POST request, it will either edit or create a new to-do item.

Since the Tornado web server uses class-based views, we only need to define one class, which accepts a GET or POST request. You can refer to the source code found at chapter3/server/server.py. The full code for our server is as follows:

```python
import tornado.httpserver
import tornado.ioloop
import tornado.options
import tornado.web

import pymongo
from bson.objectid import ObjectId
from tornado_cors import CorsMixin
from tornado.options import define, options
import json
define("port", default=8000, help="run on the given port",
  type=int)

class Application(tornado.web.Application):
    def __init__(self):
        handlers = [(r"/todos", Todos)]
        conn = pymongo.Connection("localhost")
        self.db = conn["todos"]
        settings = dict(
            xsrf_cookies=False,
            debug=True
        )
        tornado.web.Application.__init__(self, handlers,
          **settings)

class Todos(CorsMixin, tornado.web.RequestHandler):
    CORS_ORIGIN = '*'
    CORS_METHODS = 'POST,GET,OPTIONS'
    CORS_HEADERS = 'Origin, X-Requested-With, Content-Type,
      Accept, content-type'
    CORS_MAX_AGE = 1728000
```

```python
CORS_CREDENTIALS = False
def get(self):


    Todos = self.application.db.todos
    todo_id = self.get_argument("id", None)

    if todo_id:
        todo = Todos.find_one({"_id": ObjectId(todo_id)})
        todo["_id"] = str(todo['_id'])
        self.write(todo)
    else:
        todos = Todos.find()
        result = []
        data = {}
        for todo in todos:
            todo["_id"] = str(todo['_id'])
            result.append(todo)
        data['todos'] = result
        self.write(data)

def options(self):

    todo_id = self.get_argument("id", None)
    Todos = self.application.db.todos
    #if self.request['Access-Control-Request-Method'] ==
      'POST':
    self.set_header("Access-Control-Allow-Headers",
      "content-type")

def post(self):
    data = json.loads(self.request.body)

    Todos = self.application.db.todos
    todo_id = self.get_argument("id", None)

    if todo_id:
        # perform an edit
        todo = Todos.find_one({"_id": ObjectId(todo_id)})

        # here should perform the update...
        todo['text'] = data['text']
        todo['details'] = data['details']
        todo['done'] = data['done']
        Todos.save(todo)
```

```
            # cos _id is not JSON serializable.
            todo["_id"] = str(todo['_id'])
            self.write(todo)
        else:
            data = json.loads(self.request.body)
            todo = {
                'text': data['text'],
                'details': data['details'],
                'done': data['done']
            }

            a = Todos.insert(todo)

            # cos _id is not JSON serializable.

            todo['_id'] = str(a)
            self.write(todo)

def main():
    tornado.options.parse_command_line()
    http_server = tornado.httpserver.HTTPServer(Application())
    http_server.listen(options.port)
    tornado.ioloop.IOLoop.instance().start()

if __name__ == "__main__":
    main()
```

Here's what's happening in our code:

- Right at the top of server.py, we simply import various libraries required for our sever.

- Next, we have the Application class defined, where we initialize the handlers required for our server. Handlers are simply URLs that are mapped to class-based views in the Tornado web server.

- The Todos class contains three functions:
    - get: This function supports the GET operations
    - options: This function supports the CORS OPTIONS string
    - post: This function supports the POST operations

- Finally, we define a main() function, which is supposed to run our Tornado server when called.

To make sure that the Tornado Python server is working, you must first run
MongoDB on your computer, navigate to the folder where `server.py` resides,
and then run the following command:

```
python server.js
```

Once you issue the preceding command, open up your web browser and navigate
to `http:/localhost:8000`; you will see the following screen:

```
localhost:8000

Traceback (most recent call last):
  File "/Library/Python/2.7/site-packages/tornado/web.py", line 1134, in _execute
    self._when_complete(self.prepare(), self._execute_method)
  File "/Library/Python/2.7/site-packages/tornado/web.py", line 1693, in prepare
    raise HTTPError(self._status_code)
HTTPError: HTTP 404: Not Found
```

Getting an error since we have not defined a handler for this URL

We get an error message because we did not define any handlers for the URL at
`http://localhost:8000`. So let's now change our URL to `http://localhost:8000/`
`todos`. You should technically receive an empty page, but because we already have
some test data saved in MongoDB, you will see the following screen:

```
localhost:8000/todos

{
  - todos: [
    - {
        text: "mofo",
        _id: "536b973885f0f209516af0c3",
        done: true,
        details: "mofo"
      },
    - {
        text: "sa dsd",
        id: "536b97b085f0f20951752170",
```

A sample list of data returned

So when we perform a GET request at `/todos`, we simply retrieve a full list of to-dos.
Similarly, when we perform a GET request with an ID, you will see that only one
to-do item is being returned.

One to-do item returned

Changing AngularJS to perform RESTful requests

Now that our server is ready, we need to start coding our AngularJS app to make it ready for RESTful operations. We'll be making changes to the code found in js/controllers and js/services, in general. We'll start with js/services/todo.js first.

Using the $http module of AngularJS

Let's get back to js/services/todo.js. We are going to include four basic operations in this module, namely getting all to-do items, getting one to-do item, saving to-do lists, and finally, editing to-do item operations.

The code that will consume the RESTful APIs is as follows:

```
angular.module('todoApp.services',[])
.config(function ($httpProvider){
  $httpProvider.defaults.useXDomain = true;
  delete $httpProvider.defaults.headers.common['X-Requested-With'];
})
.factory('Todos', function($http) {
  return {
    getAll: function () {
      // return $http.get('http://10.0.2.2:8000/todos'); // if
        using android
      return $http.get('http://localhost:8000/todos');
    },
```

```
getTodo: function (id) {
  // return $http.get('http://10.0.2.2:8000/todos?id='+id); //
    if using android
  return $http.get('http://localhost:8000/todos?id='+id);
},
save: function (todoData) {
  // return $http.post('http://10.0.2.2:8000/todos',
    todoData); // if using android
  return $http.post('http://localhost:8000/todos', todoData);
},
edit: function (id, todoData) {
  // return $http.post('http://10.0.2.2:8000/todos',
    todoData); // if using android
  return $http.post('http://localhost:8000/todos?id='+id,
    todoData);
},
delete: function(id) {
  console.log(" i dont think I have a delete here.")
}
}
})
```

First and foremost, notice that we have a .config file where we used $httpProvider and made some changes to the default behavior of the AngularJS $http requests. The first two highlighted lines with .config are there to ensure that cross-domain requests can be done, since our AngularJS app resides in a different location as our server.

Secondly, notice that the services module simply returns the operations we need, with the relevant RESTful endpoints. For example, getAll is a function that returns the endpoint http://localhost:8000/todos using a GET request.

Rewriting controllers to make use of the $http module

In the previous section, we rewrote services/todo.js so that it now performs RESTful requests. How do we consume these services in the controller? We can simply do so by including Todo under the controllers that we want to use the services provided for by Todo. Take for instance, ListCtrl:

```
.controller('ListCtrl', function($scope, $rootScope, $http, Todos) {

  Todos.getAll().success(function(data) {

    $rootScope.todos = data['todos'];
```

```
  })

  $scope.remaining = function() {
    var count = 0;
    angular.forEach($scope.todos, function(todo) {
      count += todo.done ? false : true;
    });
    return count;
  };

})
```

In the highlighted line in the preceding code, notice that we have included `Todos`. Next, in order to retrieve all to-do items, we simply make a `.getAll()` call by doing `Todos.getAll()`. If the call is successful, we return the JSON data and assign it to `$rootScope.todos`.

We use `$rootScope` instead of `$scope`, because I wanted all the controllers to be able to access the current state of `todos` without making another call to the backend server.

Next, for `CreateCtrl`, we simply make a `.save()` to the backend with our to-do data:

```
.controller('CreateCtrl', function($scope, $rootScope, $location,
  $timeout, Todos) {
    $scope.todoText = "";
    $scope.todoDetails = "";
    $scope.save = function() {
      var todo = {
        text:$scope.todoText,
        done:false,
        details:$scope.todoDetails
      };
      console.log($rootScope.todos);
      $rootScope.todos.push(todo);
      console.log($rootScope.todos);

      Todos.save(todo);
      $location.path('/');

    };
  })
```

Notice that we simply make a `Todos.save()` call to save our data to our backend server.

Finally, let's take a look at `EditCtrl`. This time around, we simply get the to-do item by its ID, and perform `edit()` when we have made changes to the item. This is shown by the highlighted line in the following code:

```
.controller('EditCtrl',
    function($scope, $location, $routeParams, Todos) {
        //$scope.todos = Todos;
        console.log($location.$$path.split("/"));
        var id = $location.$$path.split("/")[2];
        var result = Todos.getTodo(id).success(function(data) {
            console.log(" and the returned data is ");
            console.log(data);
            $scope.todoText = data.text;
            $scope.todoDetails = data.details;
            return data;
        })
        $scope.save = function() {
            var todo = {
                id:$location.$$path.split("/")[2],
                text:$scope.todoText,
                details:$scope.todoDetails,
                done:true
            }

            Todos.edit(id, todo);

        }
    });
```

Checking our code

Now that we have rewritten our AngularJS app, it's time to check if it works correctly. As usual, fire up your server by issuing the Python `server.py` and start your AngularJS app using a local server. When you first load your AngularJS app, you will see a GET request on your server in the backend. Here's what it looks like on my terminal:

```
[I 140510 17:29:53 web:1635] 304 GET /todos (::1) 2.81ms
```

A GET request

Let's try creating a new to-do item by clicking on **NEW**. As usual, you should see the following screen:

Our input fields to add a to-do list

Now type in the name and details. I'm going to just type `hello world` as the name and `hello world description` as the details. Once done, click on **Save**. You should see that you are now redirected to the page containing the list of todos with the new to-do item at the bottom.

If you look at your terminal, you will also see the following screen:

```
[I 140510 17:33:44 web:1635] 200 OPTIONS /todos (::1) 0.54ms
[I 140510 17:33:44 web:1635] 304 GET /todos (::1) 5.16ms
[I 140510 17:33:44 web:1635] 200 POST /todos (::1) 1.65ms
```

A series of HTTP requests coming from our AngularJS app

The `OPTIONS` request is sent from AngularJS. You are then redirected back to the home page (that's where the `GET` request occurs), and finally, the `POST` action is completed, as shown by the last line in this terminal.

Now you can attempt to perform an edit operation. We will edit the item that we have just added:

Adding a to-do item

We will now add new details to the to-do item:

Making changes to the to-do item

Now click on **Save**. We will see the following screen when we are redirected back to the home page:

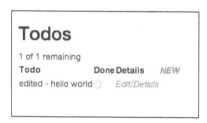

The to-do item is being edited and is reflected on the list of to-do items

If everything works as expected, we can now test our code on Android and iOS.

Preparing for PhoneGap

As usual, we will need to transfer the code that we have written under /www. Make sure you transfer the code correctly to PhoneGap. If you've done it correctly, your PhoneGap folder should look as follows:

Code arrangement at this point in time

If you have performed the previous steps, let's test it out on iOS and Android.

Testing our code on iOS

To test our code on iOS, we simply navigate to our PhoneGap project (`phonegap/todo`) and issue the following command:

```
cordova emulate ios
```

Remember to turn on your server and MongoDB as well. You should see the following screen on your Android emulator:

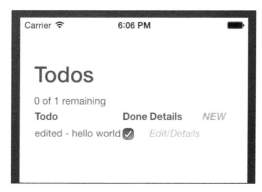

Your to-do list app should look and work as expected

This is simply some of the data that we created beforehand. Let's go ahead and create a new to-do item:

Your to-do list app should look and work as expected

Now go ahead and save it. You will see the following screen:

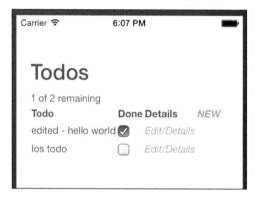

Your to-do list app should look and work as expected; creating a to-do item works

I'm just going to go ahead and edit the latest to-do item:

Editing a to-do item should work as expected

Now click on **Save**. You should see the latest item saved as shown in the following screenshot:

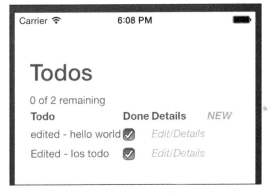

After editing and saving the to-do item, the app works as expected

Testing our code on Android

We need to make some changes in order to test our code on Android. We also need to make changes to the endpoint that we are calling; `http://localhost:8000` will need to be changed to `http://10.0.2.2`.

For this Android version, your `js/services/todo.js` will look as follows:

```
angular.module('todoApp.services',[])
.config(function ($httpProvider){
  $httpProvider.defaults.useXDomain = true;
  delete $httpProvider.defaults.headers.common
    ['X-Requested-With'];
})
.factory('Todos', function($http) {
  return {
    getAll: function () {
      return $http.get('http://10.0.2.2:8000/todos'); // if using
        android
      //return $http.get('http://localhost:8000/todos');
    },
    getTodo: function (id) {
      return $http.get('http://10.0.2.2:8000/todos?id='+id);
        // if using android
      //return $http.get('http://localhost:8000/todos?id='+id);
    },
```

```
    save: function (todoData) {
      return $http.post('http://10.0.2.2:8000/todos', todoData);
        // if using android
      //return $http.post('http://localhost:8000/todos',
        todoData);
    },
    edit: function (id, todoData) {
      return $http.post('http://10.0.2.2:8000/todos', todoData);
        // if using android
      //return $http.post('http://localhost:8000/todos?id='+id,
        todoData);
    },
    delete: function(id) {
      console.log(" i dont think I have a delete here.")
    }
  }
}
})
```

Notice that we are commenting out the `http://localhost:8000` version and using the `http://10.0.2.2` version.

Next, we simply navigate to our PhoneGap project `phonegap/todo` and issue the following command:

cordova emulate android

Remember to turn on your server and MongoDB as well. You should see the following screen on your Android emulator:

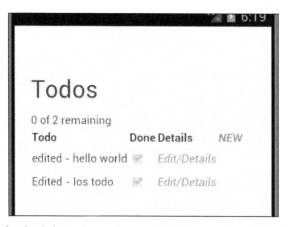

On the first load, the to-do app shows a list of items we have in the database

This is simply just some of the data that we have created beforehand. As you can see, the item created on iOS is present. So I'm just going to go ahead and create another new to-do item:

Adding a new to-do item to your Android app

Let's go ahead and save it. You should see the new item on our to-do list.

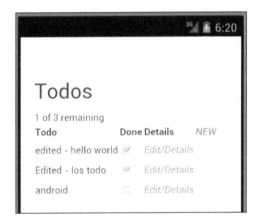

Adding a new item works as expected

Finally, I'm going to make some edits to make sure that our code is working fine. Click on **Edit/Details** for the Android item on the emulator and start editing it:

Editing a to-do item

Once you've saved the item, you will see that the Android item is now edited.

Summary

That's it! We went through quite a bit of detail in this chapter. By now you should see that shifting an AngularJS app to PhoneGap is very straightforward; all you need to do is place your files in the www/ folder. You also learned how to create RESTful apps on top of AnguarJS and the Tornado web server.

In the next chapter, we will cover advanced-level topics, such as optimizing our AngularJS app for touch devices, using PhoneGap plugins such as the Facebook plugin, and how to create directives for our AngularJS app. See you there.

4
Adding Authentication Capabilities Using PhoneGap Plugins

In this chapter, we will be adding authentication capabilities to our to-do list app. To be specific, we are going to add Facebook Login capabilities to our app. We will start working on the web-based version of our app before porting the code over to the PhoneGap version. In the PhoneGap version, we will be leveraging on the PhoneGap plugin in order to achieve what we have done for the web-based version. The porting of code will be slightly less straightforward due to the recent changes to PhoneGap's Facebook plugin. So sit tight and see how we can add login capabilities in this chapter.

Adding Facebook Connect to the to-do list app

Adding Facebook Connect to our web-based version of the app is straightforward. You will need to sign up for a new app (or use the current one) from `https://developers.facebook.com/` and take note of the app ID and app's secret key. Then, as usual, you will need to initiate your app using some Facebook-specific JavaScript and library "namely" Facebook's JavaScript SDK.

In case you are wondering, the Facebook Connect plugin is used to perform Facebook login in PhoneGap apps.

Initializing and preparing for Facebook Connect

Let's quickly dive into the source code for `index.html`:

```
<!doctype html>
<html ng-app="todoApp">
  <head>
    <link rel="stylesheet" href="http://netdna.bootstrapcdn.com/
bootstrap/3.0.3/css/bootstrap.min.css">

    <style>
    body {
      padding: 40px 20px 0 20px;
    }
    </style>

  </head>
  <body>
  <div id="fb-root"></div>
  <script src="http://connect.facebook.net/en_US/all.js"></script>
  <script>
      FB.init({
          appId       : XXX',
          xfbml       : true,
          version     : 'v1.0'
      });
  </script>
  <h2>Todos</h2>
  <div ng-view></div>


    <script src="https://ajax.googleapis.com/ajax/libs/
angularjs/1.3.0-beta.7/angular.min.js"></script>
    <script src="https://ajax.googleapis.com/ajax/libs/
angularjs/1.3.0-beta.7/angular-resource.min.js"></script>
    <script src="https://ajax.googleapis.com/ajax/libs/
angularjs/1.3.0-beta.7/angular-route.min.js"></script>
  <script src="js/controllers/todo.js"></script>
    <script src="js/controllers/user.js"></script>
    <script src="js/services/todo.js"></script>
    <script src="js/app.js"></script>
  </body>
</html>
```

Take note of the following highlighted lines of code:

```html
<div id="fb-root"></div>
<script src="http://connect.facebook.net/en_US/all.js"></script>
<script>
    FB.init({
        appId      : 'XXX',
        xfbml      : true,
        version    : 'v1.0'
    });
</script>
```

The preceding code is basically Facebook-specific and is required in order for you to use Facebook Login for your web application. You will need to replace xxx with your own app ID, and make sure that the site URL (found under your app settings on Facebook Developers) is set to your login location.

Next, we have `<script src="js/controllers/user.js"></script>`. This will be a small snippet of code, where we will add the login capabilities for our app.

Writing the user controller

We'll now start with the controller aspect of the app. So let's start by creating a new file called `user.js` in `js/controllers/user.js`. As usual, we will need to define `angular.module` and we are going to name this controller `UserLoginCtrl`. We can simply make calls to Facebook using the FB object, which was initiated earlier in `index.html`. So here's what your `user.js` should look like:

```javascript
angular.module('todoApp.userControllers',[])

    .controller('UserLoginCtrl', function($scope, $rootScope, $http,
$location, Todos) {

    $scope.login = function() {

    // so this is for desktop testing
    FB.login(function(response) {
      if (response.authResponse) {
        console.log('Welcome!  Fetching your information.... ');
        FB.api('/me', function(response) {
          console.log('Good to see you, ' + response.name + '.');
          $location.path('/');
          if(!$scope.$$phase) $scope.$apply();
```

```
        });
      } else {
        console.log('User cancelled login or did not fully
authorize.');
      }
    });
  };
```

The main function here is `$scope.login`, which simply wraps around the `FB.login` call where we attempt to login the user. The AngularJS-specific stuff is found in the following code:

```
    $location.path('/');
    if(!$scope.$$phase) $scope.$apply();
```

This means that we will redirect the user back to the index page after he/she has logged in successfully.

 The `$apply()` option is meant to start a `$digest` cycle. A great tutorial that explains this operation is available at http://www.sitepoint. com/understanding-angulars-apply-digest/.

Now you may be wondering if there's any page where login takes place. Yes, of course, and this is exactly what we are going to do in the next section.

Adding a login page

We are going to create a new file called `login.html`. This file will reside in the `partials` folder, where all HTML snippets are found. However, first, we need to define the route where this HTML partial will be loaded. So let's take a look at `app.js`:

```
angular.module('todoApp', [
  'ngRoute',
  'todoApp.controllers',
  'todoApp.userControllers',
  'todoApp.services'
])

.config(function($routeProvider) {
```

```
$routeProvider
  .when('/', {
    controller:'ListCtrl',
    templateUrl:'partials/list.html'
  })
  .when('/edit/:id', {
    controller:'EditCtrl',
    templateUrl:'partials/detail.html'
  })
  .when('/new', {
    controller:'CreateCtrl',
    templateUrl:'partials/detail.html'
  })
  .when('/login', {
    controller:'UserLoginCtrl',
    templateUrl:'partials/login.html'
  })
  .otherwise({
    redirectTo:'/'
  });
})
```

There are two highlighted parts in our code, `todoApp.userControllers`, which means that we are loading this controller so it can be used in our app.

The second instance is the following code:

```
.when('/login', {
  controller:'UserLoginCtrl',
  templateUrl:'partials/login.html'
})
```

The preceding code means that when the route is /login, we will be using UserLoginCtrl and login.html. Now that we have defined the route and coded UserLoginCtrl, it's time to work on login.html. The login.html file is simple and straightforward; it contains a title and **Login** button:

```
<h3>Please login</h3>
<button ng-click="login()">Login</button>
```

Yup, that's right, simple and straightforward. So if you save your files and visit your app at /login, you will get the following screenshot:

Login Screen

So right now, we can try out by clicking on **Login**. If everything works correctly, you will be redirected back to your index page. This page will show you a complete list of **Todos**, as shown in the following screenshot:

List of Todos

Alright, pretty cool yeah? However, we are missing out some stuff. For example, what happens if the user wants to logout? Or what happens when the user goes straight to the index page without logging in first? We will deal with that in the next two sections.

Adding a logout function

Perform the following steps to add a `logout` function:

1. To add a `logout` functionality, we will first need to have a logout button. So, we can add this functionality in the index page by placing the logout button in `partials/list.html`:

```
<button ng-click="logout()" style="float:right">Logout</button>
<span>{{remaining()}} of {{todos.length}} remaining</span>
<table>
  <thead>
  <tr>
    <th>Todo</th>
    <th>Done</th>
    <th>Details</th>
    <th><a href="#/new"><i class="icon-plus-sign">NEW</i></a></th>
  </tr>
  </thead>
  <tbody>
  <tr ng-repeat="todo in todos">
    <td>{{todo.text}}</td>
    <td><input type="checkbox" ng-model="todo.done" value="todo._
id"></td>
    <td>
      <a href="#/edit/{{todo._id}}"><i class="icon-pencil">Edit/
Details</i></a>
    </td>
  </tr>
  </tbody>
</table>
```

2. The entire `partials/list.html` file is the same as before, except for the highlighted line where the `logout` button is added.

3. Next, since the `logout` button is found in `partials/list.html`, this means that we need to add a function to log out of `todo.js`. Now, going to `controllers/todo.js`, prepend the `$scope.logout` function just before `Todos.getAll()`:

```
$scope.logout = function () {
  alert('logging out')
  // this is the desktop version
  FB.logout(function(response) {
    alert('logged out');
```

```
     $location.path('/login');
     if(!$scope.$$phase) $scope.$apply();
   });
}


Todos.getAll().success(function(data) {
  $rootScope.todos = data['todos'];
})
```

4. The highlighted lines of code are the lines of code that will be handling the logout. So basically, what happens is that on clicking the **Logout** button, you will see an alert box that says **logged out**, after which you will be redirected to the login page.

5. Save your files and refresh your browser. You should see the following screenshot:

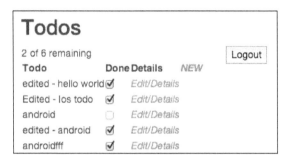

List of todos with the Logout button

6. Notice that we have a **Logout** button to the right of the page. Now click on it and you should see the following screenshot, if everything is working correctly:

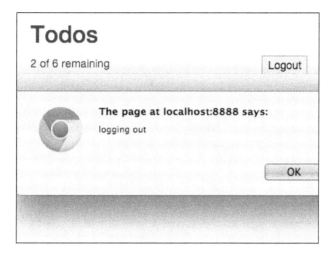

7. After clicking on **OK**, you will be redirected back to the login page.

Now, let's move on to the last requirement, which is checking for the login status.

Checking the login status

Checking of the login status will be done in the index page, for simplicity. So we need to add a function in `controllers/todo.js`. We need to prepend the functions used in the following code, before the `$scope.logout` function that we added in the previous section:

```
$scope.checkLogin = function() {
  FB.getLoginStatus(function(response) {
    if (response.status == 'connected') {
      //alert('logged in');
      console.log("logged in bro");
    }
    else {
      // alert('not logged in');
      $location.path('/login');
      if(!$scope.$$phase) $scope.$apply();
    }
  });
}
$scope.checkLogin();
```

Now save the file and refresh your browser. If you are still logged out, you should be redirected to the /login page, where you will be asked to log in. For example, as I am still logged out from the previous section, I am redirected to the login page. After clicking on the **Login** button, I am prompted to log in, as shown in the following screenshot:

Facebook Login

After entering my credentials, I am logged in successfully. Feel free to try out other functionalities that we have coded in the previous section, just to make sure that things are working as expected.

If everything is good to go, it's time to move on and port our code to PhoneGap. It will be slightly different from what we have done in the previous sections, as there are some extra steps and precautions that we have to take. You might want to take a short break before continuing to the next section.

Facebook login for PhoneGap

PhoneGap has gone through quite a bit of changes not only for the main library, but also the plugin system. In this section, you will see that we can quickly install PhoneGap plugins using the command-line tool, without the usual multiple steps that we have to follow if we want to install it manually.

Installing the Facebook plugin

Since we have already added iOS and Android platforms, this plugin installation will add plugins for both iOS and Android. To install the Facebook plugin, you will need to navigate to your `todo` app project. Next, issue the following command:

```
cordova plugin add
https://github.com/phonegap/phonegap-facebook-plugin, --variable APP_
ID="XXXXX" --variable APP_NAME="AngularPhoneGapTest".
```

You will need to replace xxxx with your app ID and you can name your `app_name` app any name you want.

The installation process is now complete. For Android, you will need three more steps:

1. Import your `todo` app into your Eclipse development environment as an Android project.

2.   While still in your Eclipse editor, in the left-hand column where all your projects are listed, right click on **Properties**.

3.   Make sure that you import `FacebookLib` and `CordovaLib` under the **Library** section (at the bottom of the next screenshot):

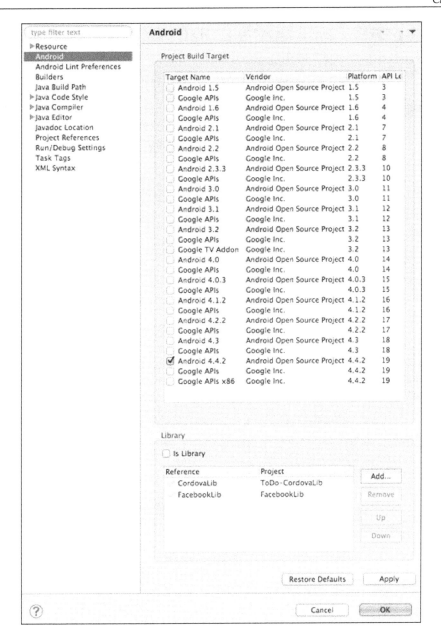

Once this is done, we have completed installation for both iOS and Android. Now, it's time to test the code. Most of the examples run on iOS, but bear in mind that the same piece of code will run properly and correctly on Android as well.

Testing out Facebook Login on PhoneGap

In order to test if our Facebook Login plugin is installed correctly on PhoneGap, we need to write a simple example just to see if the app is working correctly. There are many examples out there on the Internet, but I've written a simple one here that should quickly show if our app is working. At the same time, you will also see that calling the FB SDK is also slightly different. Let's jump straight into the code by writing a new `index.html` page for our PhoneGap app:

```html
<!DOCTYPE html>
<html>
  <head>
    </head>
  <body>
    <button onclick="login()">Login</button>

    <div id="data">loading ...</div>
    <div id="fb-root"></div>
    <!-- cordova -->
    <script src="cordova.js"></script>
    <!-- cordova facebook plugin -->
    <script src="cdv-plugin-fb-connect.js"></script>
    <!-- facebook js sdk -->
    <script src="facebook-js-sdk.js"></script>
    <script>
    if ((typeof cordova == 'undefined') && (typeof Cordova ==
'undefined')) alert('Cordova variable does not exist. Check that you
have included cordova.js correctly');

    if (typeof CDV == 'undefined') alert('CDV variable does not exist.
Check that you have included cdv-plugin-fb-connect.js correctly');

    if (typeof FB == 'undefined') alert('FB variable does not exist.
Check that you have included the Facebook JS SDK file.');

    FB.Event.subscribe('auth.login', function(response) {
                alert('auth.login event');
                });

    FB.Event.subscribe('auth.logout', function(response) {
                alert('auth.logout event');
```

```
                        });

    FB.Event.subscribe('auth.sessionChange', function(response) {
                        alert('auth.sessionChange event');
                        });

    FB.Event.subscribe('auth.statusChange', function(response) {
                        alert('auth.statusChange event');
                        });



    var fbLoginSuccess = function (userData) {
        alert("UserInfo: " + JSON.stringify(userData));
    }
    function login() {
      facebookConnectPlugin.login(["basic_info"],
          fbLoginSuccess,
          function (error) { alert("" + error) }
      );
    }



    document.addEventListener('deviceready', function() {
      try {
      alert('Device is ready! Make sure you set your app_id below this
alert.');
      FB.init({ appId: "XXXX", nativeInterface: CDV.FB,
useCachedDialogs: false });
      document.getElementById('data').innerHTML = "";
      } catch (e) {
      alert(e);
      }
      }, false);
    </script>
    <div id="log"></div>
  </body>
</html>
```

The preceding code is somewhat similar to the official examples, but with three subtle differences, as shown by the highlighted lines:

- ```
  <button onclick="login()">Login</button>
  ```

  We are only focused on `login()` here, so we will remove the remaining functionalities such as posting to the wall and so on

- The second section of the code is as follows:
  ```
  <script src="cordova.js"></script>
  <!-- cordova facebook plugin -->
  <script src="cdv-plugin-fb-connect.js"></script>
  <!-- facebook js sdk -->
  <script src="facebook-js-sdk.js"></script>
  ```

  We are still required to install all PhoneGap-related files, including those related to the Facebook plugins

- The third and most important section is as follows:
  ```
  var fbLoginSuccess = function (userData) {
      alert("UserInfo: " + JSON.stringify(userData));
  }
  function login() {
    facebookConnectPlugin.login(["basic_info"],
        fbLoginSuccess,
        function (error) { alert("" + error) }
    );
  }
  ```

Notice that we are making a login call to Facebook using `facebookConnectPlugin.login` instead of `FB.login`. This is due to the major change in plugins by the PhoneGap team. When we are porting our code to PhoneGap from the web version, our Facebook calls will be changed to reflect this. For now, follow on with this section. Once the code is written, save the file and run the iOS emulator. Issue the following command:

```
cordova emulate ios
```
```

You will then see your iOS emulator get fired up, and you will be greeted with the following screenshot:

On entering the app

After clicking on **OK**, you will see that the **loading...** message has vanished. Next, you can click on **Login** and you will be presented with Facebook's login page:

Facebook Login Screen

Since we have already authorized the app, there's no need to log in or authorize the app again. Click on **OK** and you should see a new screen with an alert box showing a JSON representation of your data:

If you get the previous screenshot, this means that everything you have done till now is right and should work well for Android too. If so, time to port our web-based version of the code to the PhoneGap version.

From web to PhoneGap

If you remember, in the previous section, I briefly mentioned that making calls to Facebook using the JavaScript SDK is now slightly different in PhoneGap, compared to the web-based version. Instead of a simplistic `FB.login()` call in the web version, we need to make a `facebookConnectPlugin.login()` call in the PhoneGap version. In this section, we'll take careful steps to port our code from the web-based version to a PhoneGap version.

Importing Facebook and PhoneGap plugins

First, we need to import Facebook- and PhoneGap-related plugins. We also need to slightly change how we initiate the FB object. So going back to your index.html file, here's what you need to do:

```html
<!doctype html>
<html ng-app="todoApp">
  <head>
    <link rel="stylesheet" href="http://netdna.bootstrapcdn.com/
bootstrap/3.0.3/css/bootstrap.min.css">
    <style>
    body {
      padding: 40px 20px 0 20px;
    }
    </style>
  </head>
  <body>
  <div id="fb-root"></div>
  <h2>Todos</h2>
  <div ng-view></div>
    <!-- this is for phonegap -->
    <script src="cordova.js"></script>
    <!-- cordova facebook plugin -->
    <script src="cdv-plugin-fb-connect.js"></script>
    <!-- facebook js sdk -->
    <script src="facebook-js-sdk.js"></script>

    <script>
    document.addEventListener('deviceready', function() {
      try {
      alert('Device is ready! Make sure you set your app_id below this
alert.');
        FB.init({ appId: "135542699836039", nativeInterface: CDV.FB,
useCachedDialogs: false });

      } catch (e) {
      alert(e);
      }
      }, false);
    </script>
    <script src="https://ajax.googleapis.com/ajax/libs/
angularjs/1.3.0-beta.7/angular.min.js"></script>
    <script src="https://ajax.googleapis.com/ajax/libs/
angularjs/1.3.0-beta.7/angular-resource.min.js"></script>
    <script src="https://ajax.googleapis.com/ajax/libs/
angularjs/1.3.0-beta.7/angular-route.min.js"></script>
```

```
    <!--
    <script src="https://ajax.googleapis.com/ajax/libs/
angularjs/1.3.0-beta.7/angular-touch.min.js"></script>
    -->
    <script src="js/controllers/todo.js"></script>
    <script src="js/controllers/user.js"></script>
    <script src="js/services/todo.js"></script>
    <script src="js/app.js"></script>
  </body>
</html>
```

You will first need to import `cordova.js`, `cdv-plugin-fb-connect.js`, and `faceboo-js-sdk.js` as shown here:

```
    <!-- this is for phonegap -->
    <script src="cordova.js"></script>
    <!-- cordova facebook plugin -->
    <script src="cdv-plugin-fb-connect.js"></script>
    <!-- facebook js sdk -->
    <script src="facebook-js-sdk.js"></script>
```

Next, we initiate the FB object by waiting for the `deviceready` event specific to PhoneGap:

```
    <script>
    document.addEventListener('deviceready', function() {
        try {
        alert('Device is ready! Make sure you set your app_id below this
alert.');
        FB.init({ appId: "XXXXX", nativeInterface: CDV.FB,
useCachedDialogs: false });

        } catch (e) {
        alert(e);
        }
        }, false);
    </script>
```

As usual, remember to replace the xxxxx with your own app ID from Facebook so that your login redirects correctly, and has the right credentials.

Changing FB to facebookConnectPlugin

The next thing that we need to do is change FB to facebookConnectPlugin. We will start with controller/user.js. The code should look like the following, after the change:

```
angular.module('todoApp.userControllers',[])

  .controller('UserLoginCtrl', function($scope, $rootScope, $http,
$location, Todos) {


    $scope.login = function() {
      // place where the user just click and login
      var fbLoginSuccess = function(userData) {
        alert("UserInfo: " + JSON.stringify(userData));
$location.path('/');
        if(!$scope.$$phase) $scope.$apply();

      }



      // this is used for PhoneGaP ver
      facebookConnectPlugin.login(["basic_info"],
        fbLoginSuccess,
        function (error) { alert("" + error) }
    );


    };

  })
```

We have a new variable named fbLoginSuccess, which is called after the user logs in successfully. Next, we have facebookConnectPlugin.login, which makes a call to log in to Facebook via PhoneGap's plugin.

Next, we need to work on `controller.js`. The two functions that you need to change are `$scope.checkLogin` and `$scope.logout`. We simply replace FB with `facebookConnectPlugin`. So here's what the code looks like now:

```
$scope.checkLogin = function() {
    facebookConnectPlugin.getLoginStatus(function(response) {
        alert(response);
        if (response.status == 'connected') {
            //alert('logged in');
            console.log("logged in bro");
            $location.path('/');
            if(!$scope.$$phase) $scope.$apply();
        }
        else {
            // alert('not logged in');
            $location.path('/login');
            if(!$scope.$$phase) $scope.$apply();
        }
    });

}
$scope.logout = function () {
    alert('logging out')

    // this is the PhoneGap version
    facebookConnectPlugin.logout(function(response) {
        alert('logged out');
        $location.path('/login');
        if(!$scope.$$phase) $scope.$apply();
    });

}
```

Now that we have made the required changes, it's time that we test the functionalities.

The to-do list app with Facebook Login on PhoneGap

As usual, we need to run our code using PhoneGap's command-line interface. So to change your current directory back to the to do list app, issue the following command:

```
cordova build ios
cordova emulate ios
```

Once you have issued the command, you should see your iOS emulator fired up. Next, you will see the following screenshot:

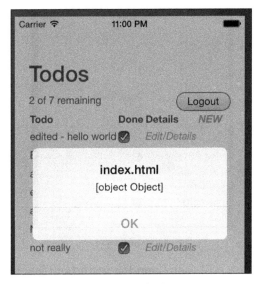

On Entering the App

As we are still logged in from the previous sections, we get to see our to-do list items even after clicking on **OK**. At this point, if you are still logged in, feel free to click on **Logout**, after which you should see the following screenshot:

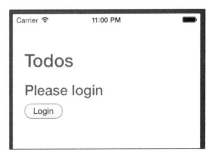

Login Screen

As usual, you can log in and be greeted by the previous screenshot. After clicking on **OK**, you can start to play around with your app.

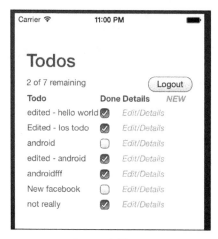

Successful login

Feel free to add new items, edit them, and log in and out just to see if the code is working correctly. If all goes well, congratulations! You now have a working PhoneGap app making RESTful calls coupled with Facebook Login capabilities.

Summary

To summarize, we worked our way from a very simple AngularJS app to one which can make RESTful calls coupled with Facebook Login capabilities. At each stage, we also ported the code to PhoneGap and made sure it works. The important takeaway here, is that using a command-line interface can drastically reduce the number of steps required to set up our PhoneGap project. In the next chapter, we will be working on animations; various animation techniques will be used for our PhoneGap app.

5
Sprucing Up the App Using Animations and Mobile Design

Welcome to this chapter! In this chapter, we will spruce up our app using animation and styles that mimic the mobile user interface. This will be a short yet useful chapter. As usual, the code shown in this chapter can be applied across iOS and Android apps.

In this chapter, we'll learn about:

- Performing animations using ngAnimate
- Pitfalls to avoid when performing animations in PhoneGap

Adding animations to your web app

Adding animations is surprisingly easy using AngularJS. The ngAnimate module of AngularJS will take users there with CSS animations.

We'll start by adding animation to our web app before porting it over to PhoneGap. To do this, head back to your web-based version of the code and open `index.html`. There are three changes that you need to make:

1. Add a new `index.css` file.
2. Add `class="todos"` in your `<div ng-view> </div>`.
3. Add `<script src="https://ajax.googleapis.com/ajax/libs/angularjs/1.3.0-beta.7/angular-animate.min.js"></script>` to the list of imported JavaScript.

4. The end result of your code in `index.html` should look like this:

```html
<!doctype html>
<html ng-app="todoApp">
  <head>
    <link rel="stylesheet"
      href="http://netdna.bootstrapcdn.com/bootstrap/
      3.0.3/css/bootstrap.min.css">
    <link rel="stylesheet" href="css/index.css">
    <style>
    body {
      padding: 40px 20px 0 20px;
    }
    </style>

  </head>
  <body>
  <div id="fb-root"></div>
  <script src="http://connect.facebook.net/en_US/all.js"></script>
  <script>
      FB.init({
          appId      : 'XXXXX',
          xfbml      : true,
          version    : 'v1.0'
      });
  </script>
  <h2>Todos</h2>
  <div ng-view class="todos"></div>

    <script src="https://ajax.googleapis.com/
      ajax/libs/angularjs/1.3.0-beta.7/angular.min.js"></script>
    <script src="https://ajax.googleapis.com/ajax/libs/
      angularjs/1.3.0-beta.7/angular-resource.min.js"></script>
    <script src="https://ajax.googleapis.com/ajax/libs/
      angularjs/1.3.0-beta.7/angular-route.min.js"></script>
    <script src="https://ajax.googleapis.com/ajax/libs/
      angularjs/1.3.0-beta.7/angular-animate.min.js"></script>
  <script src="js/controllers/todo.js"></script>
    <script src="js/controllers/user.js"></script>
    <script src="js/services/todo.js"></script>
    <script src="js/app.js"></script>
  </body>
</html>
```

The highlighted lines of code are the ones that you need to add to `index.html`. You may have noticed that we have not created `index.css`; that's what we are going to do right now:

1. Open your editor, create a new file in the `css` folder, and name it `index.css`. We are going to create the initial state of `todos` and define how the animation will look. Our goal is to make our app slide in from the left on initialization. Clicking on **Edit/Details** or **New** should shift it towards the right. By clicking on **Cancel**, the screen should shift leftwards. Our `index.css` file should look like the following:

```
.todos {
    position: absolute;
    background: coral;
    display: block;
    width:90%;
    border-left:1px solid black;
}

.todos.ng-enter, .todos.ng-leave {
  transition: 500ms ease-in all;
}

.todos.ng-enter.ng-enter-active, .todos.ng-leave {
  left: 0;
}
.todos.ng-leave.ng-leave-active, .todos.ng-enter {
  left: 200%;
}
```

The `.todos` class simply defines the initial state of the `todos` class. Next, we have `.todos.ng-enter` and `.todos.ng-leave`, where we define a transition time of `500ms` and an ease-in effect.

2. Next comes the fun part. `.todos.ng-enter.ng-enter-active, .todos.ng-leave` is defined as `left:0`, which means that on entering a new route, the partial in question will shift in from right to left till the distance from the left side of the parent div is 0 px.

3. Similarly, on leaving, it is defined by `.todos.ng-leave.ng-leave-active, .todos.ng-enter` at `left:200%`.

So what are we doing here ? If you noticed, we first defined `<div ng-view >` with `class="todos"`, and then we attached AngularJS specific animations by using `ng-enter`, `ng-leave`, `ng-enter-active`, and `ng-leave-active`. These are the four basic states that you can define for an animation.

4. Now save the file and open `index.html` on your favorite web browser. Please remember to run your server and the MongoDB server in order for this app to work. You should be greeted with the following screen:

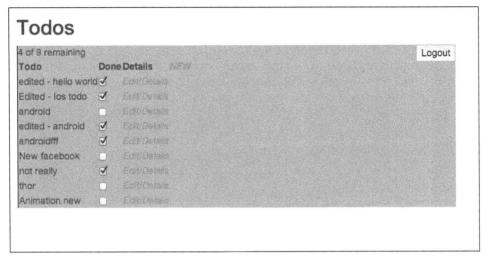

The Todos list app

5. Click on **NEW** or **Edit/Details** and you should see animations shifting in from right or left, depending on whether you cancel the action or not. For instance, you can click on **Edit/Details** first and make sure that you are moving towards the right with a new screen as follows:

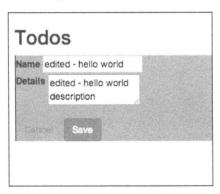

Making changes to our items and should work
as expected with animation effects

6. If you click on **Cancel**, you will see your screen shift leftwards, which is a direction that you would expect.

As soon as you get the preceding result, you know that all is working right. It's time to add in CSS styles that mimic the usual mobile user interface.

Adding mobile CSS styles to your app

In order to further spruce up our app, we will be leveraging on the CSS libraries of TopCoat. You can get TopCoat CSS libraries from `http://topcoat.io/`. We also need to change our `index.html` file a bit more in order to leverage on the styles provided by TopCoat.

1. For a start, replace the stylesheet which points to Bootstrap CDN with the following code:

```
<link rel="stylesheet" href="//cdnjs.cloudflare.com/ajax/libs/
    topcoat/0.8.0/css/topcoat-mobile-light.css">
```

2. After this, just before `<div ng-view class="todos"></div>`, prepend the following code:

```
<div class="topcoat-navigation-bar">
    <div class="topcoat-navigation-bar__item center full">
        <h1 class="topcoat-navigation-bar__title">Todos</h1>
    </div>
</div>
```

This is to give a universal header that we commonly see in mobile apps.

After these changes, your `index.html` file should look like this:

```
<!doctype html>
<html ng-app="todoApp">
  <head>
    <link rel="stylesheet" href="//cdnjs.cloudflare.com/ajax/
      libs/topcoat/0.8.0/css/topcoat-mobile-light.css">
    <link rel="stylesheet" href="css/index.css">
  </head>
  <body>
  <div id="fb-root"></div>
  <script src="http://connect.facebook.net/en_US/
    all.js"></script>
  <script>
      FB.init({
          appId      : 'XXX',
          xfbml      : true,
          version    : 'v1.0'
      });
  </script>
  <div class="topcoat-navigation-bar">
      <div class="topcoat-navigation-bar__item center full">
          <h1 class="topcoat-navigation-bar__title">Todos</h1>
      </div>
  </div>
```

```
<div ng-view class="todos"></div>


    <script src="https://ajax.googleapis.com/ajax/libs/
      angularjs/1.3.0-beta.7/angular.min.js"></script>
    <script src="https://ajax.googleapis.com/ajax/libs/
      angularjs/1.3.0-beta.7/angular-
      resource.min.js"></script>
    <script src="https://ajax.googleapis.com/ajax/libs/
      angularjs/1.3.0-beta.7/angular-
      route.min.js"></script>
    <script src="https://ajax.googleapis.com/ajax/libs/
      angularjs/1.3.0-beta.7/angular-
      animate.min.js"></script>
    <script src="https://ajax.googleapis.com/ajax/libs/
      angularjs/1.3.0-beta.7/angular-touch.min.js"></script>
    <script src="js/controllers/todo.js"></script>
    <script src="js/controllers/user.js"></script>
    <script src="js/services/todo.js"></script>
    <script src="js/app.js"></script>
  </body>
</html>
```

3. There's still one more thing we need to change, and that is the listing of `todos`. So, in `partials/list.html`, we need to change the stylistic elements so that it appears correctly when shown on a mobile device. We are simply applying TopCoat CSS classes here:

```
<div class="topcoat-list__container scroller">
  <a style="padding-left:10px" href="#/new">
    <i class="icon-plus-sign">NEW</i></a>
  <span style="padding-left:10px">
    {{remaining()}} of {{todos.length}} remaining
  </span>
  <button ng-click="logout()"
    style="position:absolute;right:10px;">Logout</button>
  <ul class="topcoat-list list">
    <li ng-repeat="todo in todos"
      class="topcoat-list__item">
      <a style="display:block; padding-left:10px"
        href="#/edit/{{todo._id}}">{{todo.text}}</a>
    </li>
  </ul>
</div>>
```

4. The next and the final step before we test our app on the browser is to remove certain parts of `index.css` so that our self-defined styles do not get confused with TopCoat CSS styles.

5. In your `index.css` file, look for `.todos` and remove `background:coral` and `border-left: 1px solid black`. So, your final `index.css` file should look like this:

```
.todos {
    position: absolute;
    display: block;
    width:100%;
}

.todos.ng-enter, .todos.ng-leave {
  transition: 500ms ease-in all;
}

.todos.ng-enter.ng-enter-active, .todos.ng-leave {
  left: 0;
}
.todos.ng-leave.ng-leave-active, .todos.ng-enter {
  left: 200%;
}
```

6. Now, open your new `index.html` file in your browser. You should see something like the following screenshot:

A mobile app with universal header

Once you have this result, you might want to play around with it to see if it is working out as expected.

Porting your web app to PhoneGap

Now we are at the final step, which is porting our app to PhoneGap. The steps are very similar to the previous chapters: we need to include the required PhoneGap and Facebook plugins. Most importantly, we need to include the ngTouch module of AngularJS. Here's how our index.html file should look for our PhoneGap's version:

```html
<!doctype html>
<html ng-app="todoApp">
  <head>
    <link rel="stylesheet" href="http://cdnjs.cloudflare.com/ajax/
      libs/topcoat/0.8.0/css/topcoat-mobile-light.css">
    <link rel="stylesheet" href="css/index.css">
  </head>
  <body>
  <div id="fb-root"></div>
  <div class="topcoat-navigation-bar">
      <div class="topcoat-navigation-bar__item center full">
          <h1 class="topcoat-navigation-bar__title">Todos</h1>
      </div>
  </div>
  <div ng-view class="todos"></div>
<!-- this is for phonegap -->
    <script src="cordova.js"></script>
    <!-- cordova facebook plugin -->
    <script src="cdv-plugin-fb-connect.js"></script>
    <!-- facebook js sdk -->
    <script src="facebook-js-sdk.js"></script>

    <script>
    document.addEventListener('deviceready', function() {
      try {
      alert('Device is ready! Make sure you set your app_id below
        this alert.');
      FB.init({ appId: "XXXX", nativeInterface: CDV.FB,
        useCachedDialogs: false });

      } catch (e) {
```

```
            alert(e);
        }
    }, false);
</script>
<script src="https://ajax.googleapis.com/ajax/libs/angularjs/
    1.3.0-beta.7/angular.min.js"></script>
<script src="https://ajax.googleapis.com/ajax/libs/angularjs/
    1.3.0-beta.7/angular-resource.min.js"></script>
<script src="https://ajax.googleapis.com/ajax/libs/angularjs/
    1.3.0-beta.7/angular-route.min.js"></script>
<script src="https://ajax.googleapis.com/ajax/libs/angularjs/
    1.3.0-beta.7/angular-animate.min.js"></script>

<script src="https://ajax.googleapis.com/ajax/libs/angularjs/
    1.3.0-beta.7/angular-touch.min.js"></script>

<script src="js/controllers/todo.js"></script>
<script src="js/controllers/user.js"></script>
<script src="js/services/todo.js"></script>
<script src="js/app.js"></script>
</body>
</html>
```

It's generally the final version as per the previous section; but the initialization for PhoneGap and Facebook is included in this version. As usual, remember to use your own app ID for this file.

We also need to convert our controllers to use the PhoneGap version for Facebook API calls that we previously coded for. In the source code provided with this book, you will see that there are two code blocks for each of the functions: one for the desktop/web version and the other is for the PhoneGap version.

As mentioned in *Chapter 4, Adding Authentication Capabilities Using PhoneGap Plugins*, the PhoneGap version connects to Facebook using the `facebookConnectPlugin` namespace instead of the usual `FB` namespace (compared to previous versions).

Testing your app on iOS

To test your app on iOS, run the following commands from the root of your app's directory:

```
cordova build ios
```

```
cordova emulate ios
```

You should see the following output in your iOS emulator:

The to-do list app on iOS

In my case, I have some items left in my database and hence that's what I got in my emulator. Feel free to click around, add new items, edit them, or log in and out. It should work as expected, with animations built in.

Testing your app on Android

Now that we have tested on iOS, it's time to get your app tested on Android as well. Note that since Android reads the `http://localhost` address differently, you will need to change `http://localhost:8000` to `http://10.0.2.2:8000` at `services/todo.js` in order for the code to work.

Also, remember to change your `facebookConnectPlugin` namespace to the usual `FB` namespace in order for the Facebook Connect plugin to work.

Once that is done, you should issue the following command:

```
cordova build android
cordova emulate android
```

Your app should be working as expected.

Summary

To sum up, we created animations for our app and also made use of TopCoat CSS skins to give our app a mobile look. There are many other areas that we can improve on, such as it's design or even use other frameworks such as the Ionic framework; notice that we did not make use of the popular jQuery Mobile, since we wanted to make use of AngularJS as much as possible. Most importantly, by now you should see that the code bases for both iOS and Android are almost the same, with the exception of changing the URL of our server's location. In the next and final chapter, you will learn about distributing and getting ready to launch our mobile apps.

6
Getting Ready to Launch

In this final chapter, we will run through some of the stuff that you should be doing before launching your app to the world, whether it's through Apple App Store or Google Android Play Store.

We will be covering the following topics:

- Testing your app on your device for real
- How to change the artwork for your app
- Deploying `server.py`

We will also discuss other useful tips before you launch the app in the real world, and we'll start by launching `server.py`.

Deploying server.py

To deploy `server.py`, you will need access to an actual server. It can be rented from Amazon EC2, Linode, or DigitalOcean. The operation system I am using here is Ubuntu 12.04, although older variants of Ubuntu can work too, which include 10.04 and 11.04. Since the server is essentially a Tornado app, you will need to prepend `sudo` to every command that follows in this section, if you are not running it as root.

1. To start off, you will need to put SSH into your server and start installing the required tools and dependencies:

```
apt-get install python-setuptools
easy_install pip
pip install tornado
```

2. You will also need to install MongoDB:

```
sudo apt-key adv --keyserver hkp://keyserver.ubuntu.com:80 --recv
7F0CEB10
```

```
echo 'deb http://downloads-distro.mongodb.org/repo/ubuntu-upstart
dist 10gen' | sudo tee /etc/apt/sources.list.d/mongodb.list
```

3. Reload the local package database:

```
apt-get update
```

4. Install the MongoDB packages:

```
apt-get install mongodb-org
```

For the latest instructions on installing MongoDB, refer to `http://docs.mongodb.org/manual/tutorial/install-mongodb-on-ubuntu/`.

5. Next, make a directory for you to host your app:

```
mkdir /srv/www/
```

```
mkdir /srv/www/app_name
```

6. Now, you can simply create a file called `server.py` under `/srv/www/app_name` and copy the contents of `server.py`, which we coded in the previous sections. However, before we run `server.py` we need to install one more package:

```
pip install tornado-cors
```

7. Now that you have installed our required packages, you can run the server by issuing the following command:

```
python server.py -host=80
```

8. To check if the server is working, go to `http://XXX.XX.XX/todos` and see if you get an empty list. Your server should also show a GET response.

At this point, should you want to test your web app or PhoneGap version of the app, you have to update `js/services/todo.js` so that the URLs reflect the new IP address or domain name of the app.

There are other ways to set up `server.py`, such as using nginx and supervisor. For more details, feel free to check out the guides provided by DigitalOcean (`https://www.digitalocean.com/`) and Linode (`https://www.linode.com/`) for more details.

Now that we are done with `server.py`, it's time to move on to the apps.

Using phonegap.com

The services on `https://build.phonegap.com/` are a straightforward way for you to get your app compiled for various devices. While this is a paid service, there is a free plan if you only have one app that you want to work on. This would be fine in our case, for this chapter.

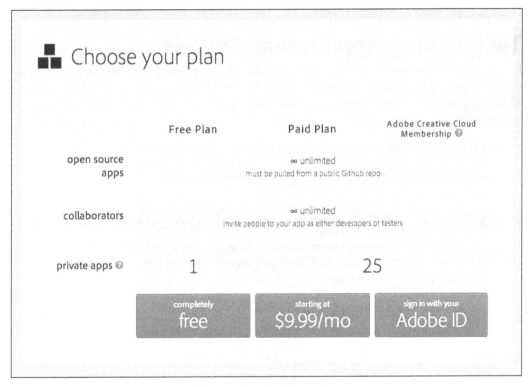

Choose a plan from PhoneGap

You will need to have an Adobe ID in order to use PhoneGap services. If not, feel free to create one. Since the process for generating compiled apps from PhoneGap may change, it's that you visit `https://build.phonegap.com/` and sign up for their services and follow their instructions.

Preparing your PhoneGap app for an Android release

This section generally focuses on things that are specific for the Android platform. This is by no means a comprehensive checklist, but some of the common tasks that you should go through before releasing your app to the Android world.

Testing your app on real devices

For most of this book, we tested our app on the Android emulator. It is always good to run your app on an actual handset to see how the app is working. To run your PhoneGap app on a real device, issue the following command after you plug your handset into your computer:

```
cordova run android
```

You will see that your app now runs on your handset.

Exporting your app to install on other devices

In the previous section we talked about installing your app on your device. What if you want to export the APK so that you can test the app on other devices? Here's what you can do:

- As usual, build your app using `cordova build android`
- Alternatively, if you can, run `cordova build release`

The previous step will create an unsigned release APK at `/path_to_your_project/platforms/android/ant-build`. This app is called `YourAppName-release-unsigned.apk`.

Now, you can simply copy `YourAppName-release-unsigned.apk` and install it on any android based device you want.

Preparing promotional artwork for release

In general, you will need to include screenshots of your app for upload to Google Play. In case your device does not allow you to take screenshots, here's what you can do:

- The first technique that you can use is to simply run your app in the emulator and take screenshots off it. The size of the screenshot may be substantially larger, so you can crop it using GIMP or some other online image resizer.

- Alternatively, use the web app version and open it in your Google Chrome Browser. Resize your browser window so that it is narrow enough to resemble the width of mobile devices.

Building your app for release

To build your app for release, you will need Eclipse IDE.

1. To start your Eclipse IDE, navigate to **File | New | Project**.

2. Next, navigate to **Existing Code | Android | Android Project**.

3. Click on **Browse** and select the root directory of your app. The **Project to Import** window should show **platforms/android**.

4. Now, select **Copy projects into workspace** if you want and then click on **Finish**.

Signing the app

We have previously exported the app (unsigned) so that we can test it on devices other than those plugged into our computer. However, to release your app to the Play Store, you need to sign them with keys. The steps here are the general steps that you need to follow in order to generate "signed" APK apps to upload your app to the Play Store.

1. Right-click on the project that you have imported in the previous section, and then navigate to **Android Tools | Export Signed Application Package**. You will see the **Project Checks** dialog.

2. In the **Project Checks** dialog, you will see if your project has any errors or not.

3. Next, you should see the **Keystore selection** dialog. You will now create the key using the app name (without space) and the extension `.keystore`. Since this app is the first version, there is no prior original name to use. Now, you can browse to the location and save the keystore, and in the same box, give the name of the keystore. In the **Keystore election** dialog, add your desired password twice and click on **Next**. You will now see the **Key Creation** dialog.

4. In the **Key Creation** dialog, use `app_name` as your alias (without any spaces) and give the password of your keystore. Feel free to enter 50 for validity (which means the password is valid for 50 years). The remaining fields such as names, organization, and so on are pretty straightforward, so you can just go ahead and fill them in.

5. Finally, select the **Destination APK** file, which is the location to which you will export your `.apk` file.

Bear in mind that the preceding steps are not a comprehensive list of instructions. For the official documentation, feel free to visit `http://developer.android.com/tools/publishing/app-signing.html`.

Now that we are done with Android, it's time to prepare our app for iOS.

iOS

As you might already know, preparing your PhoneGap app for Apple App Store requires similar levels, if not more, as compared to your usual Android deployment. In this section, I will not be covering things like making sure your app is in tandem with Apple User Interface guidelines, but rather, how to improve your app before it reaches the App Store. Before we get started, there are some basic requirements:

- Apple Developer Membership (if you ultimately want to deploy to the App Store)
- Xcode

Running your app on an iOS device

If you already have an iOS device, all you need to do is to plug your iOS device to your computer and issue the following command:

```
cordova run ios
```

You should see that your PhoneGap app will build and launch on your device. Note that before running the preceding command, you will need to install the `ios-deploy` package. You can install it using the following command:

```
sudo npm install -g ios-deploy
```

Other techniques

There are other ways to test and deploy your apps. These methods can be useful if you want to deploy your app to your own devices or even for external device testing.

Using Xcode

Now let's get started with Xcode:

1. After starting your project using the command-line tool and after adding in iOS platform support, you may actually start developing using Xcode. You can start your Xcode and click on **Open Other**, as shown in the following screenshot:

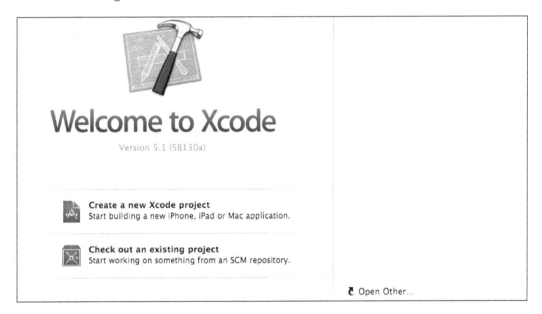

2. Once you have clicked on **Open Other**, you will need to browse to your **ToDo** app folder.

3. Drill down until you see **ToDo.xcodeproj** (navigate to **platforms | ios**). Select and open this file.

4. You will see your Xcode device importing the files. After it's all done, you should see something like the following screenshot:

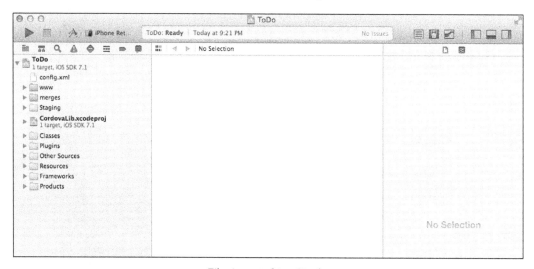

Files imported into Xcode

5. Notice that all the files are now imported to your Xcode, and you can start working from here. You can also deploy your app either to devices or simulators:

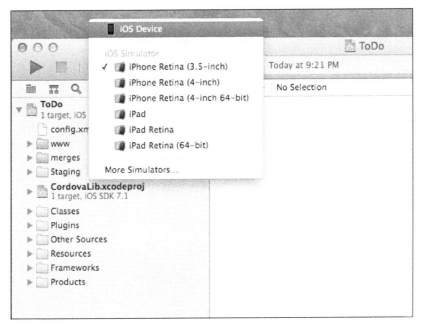

Deploy on your device or on simulators

Summary

In this chapter, we went through the basics of packaging your app before submission to the respective app stores. That's it for this book. We have covered quite a bit in this book in six chapters. In general, you should have a good idea of how to develop AngularJS apps and apply mobile skins on them so that it can be used on PhoneGap. You should also notice that developing for PhoneGap apps typically takes the pattern of creating a web app first, before converting it to a PhoneGap version. Of course, you may structure your project so that you can build a PhoneGap version from day one, but it may make testing more difficult. Anyway, I hope that you enjoyed this book and feel free to follow me at http://www.liangeugene.com and http://growthsnippets.com.

References

The following are some common resources that you can use for reference.

AngularJS and related libraries

- The main AngularJS is available at `https://angularjs.org/`; here you can learn about the basic functionalities of AngularJS
- A list of popular add-ons, modules, and plugins for AngularJS is available at `http://ngmodules.org/`
- CanJS, a framework that makes developing complex applications simple and fast is available at `http://canjs.com/`
- Ember.js, a framework that incorporates common idioms so that developers can focus on what makes your app special, is available at `http://emberjs.com/`
- Knockout is a framework that developers can use to build single page applications, custom bindings, and so it is available at `http://knockoutjs.com/`

PhoneGap and related references

- The PhoneGap main website is available at `http://phonegap.com/`
- PhoneGap Plugins are available at `https://build.phonegap.com/plugins`
- The Apache Cordova main website is available at `http://cordova.apache.org/`
- The Android Developers main website is available at `http://developer.android.com/index.html`

Others

- The iOS main website is available at `https://developer.apple.com/devcenter/ios/index.action`
- The Facebook login page is available at `https://developers.facebook.com/docs/facebook-login/v2.0`
- Facebook PhoneGap plugin is available at `https://github.com/phonegap/phonegap-facebook-plugin`
- The Ionic framework is available at `http://ionicframework.com/`

Other tutorials

In addition to the previous links, here are some useful tutorials regarding the use of AngularJS and PhoneGap. Though some of them are slightly outdated (especially for PhoneGap), it is still generally useful for you to understand how both PhoneGap and AngularJS work together by referring to the following links:

- How to use PhoneGap and AngularJS together is available at `http://tech.pro/tutorial/1336/phonegap-and-angularjs-the-start`
- Sample Mobile Application with AngularJS and PhoneGap is available at `http://coenraets.org/blog/2013/11/sample-mobile-application-with-angularjs/`
- Sample Mobile Application with Ionic Framework and PhoneGap is available at `http://coenraets.org/blog/2014/02/sample-mobile-application-with-ionic-and-angularjs/`

Index

Todos class 43
TopCoat CSS libraries
  URL 85
tornado-cor
  URL 40
Tornado Framework
  URL 40

U

user controller, Facebook Connect
  writing 59, 60

W

web
  to PhoneGap 74
web app
  animations, adding 81-84
  porting, to PhoneGap 88, 89
  testing, on Android 91
  testing, on iOS 90

X

Xcode
  using 99-101

Thank you for buying
PhoneGap and AngularJS for Cross-Platform Development

About Packt Publishing

Packt, pronounced 'packed', published its first book "*Mastering phpMyAdmin for Effective MySQL Management*" in April 2004 and subsequently continued to specialize in publishing highly focused books on specific technologies and solutions.

Our books and publications share the experiences of your fellow IT professionals in adapting and customizing today's systems, applications, and frameworks. Our solution based books give you the knowledge and power to customize the software and technologies you're using to get the job done. Packt books are more specific and less general than the IT books you have seen in the past. Our unique business model allows us to bring you more focused information, giving you more of what you need to know, and less of what you don't.

Packt is a modern, yet unique publishing company, which focuses on producing quality, cutting-edge books for communities of developers, administrators, and newbies alike. For more information, please visit our website: www.packtpub.com.

About Packt Open Source

In 2010, Packt launched two new brands, Packt Open Source and Packt Enterprise, in order to continue its focus on specialization. This book is part of the Packt Open Source brand, home to books published on software built around Open Source licenses, and offering information to anybody from advanced developers to budding web designers. The Open Source brand also runs Packt's Open Source Royalty Scheme, by which Packt gives a royalty to each Open Source project about whose software a book is sold.

Writing for Packt

We welcome all inquiries from people who are interested in authoring. Book proposals should be sent to author@packtpub.com. If your book idea is still at an early stage and you would like to discuss it first before writing a formal book proposal, contact us; one of our commissioning editors will get in touch with you.

We're not just looking for published authors; if you have strong technical skills but no writing experience, our experienced editors can help you develop a writing career, or simply get some additional reward for your expertise.

PhoneGap 3 Beginner's Guide

ISBN: 9781782160984   Paperback: 308 pages

A guide to building cross-platform apps using the W3C standards-based Cordova/PhoneGap framework

1. Understand the fundamentals of cross-platform mobile application development from build to distribution.

2. Learn to implement the most common features of modern mobile applications.

3. Take advantage of native mobile device capabilities—including the camera, geolocation, and local storage—using HTML, CSS, and JavaScript.

PhoneGap 3.x Mobile Application Development HOTSHOT

ISBN: 9781783287925   Paperback: 450 pages

Create useful and exciting real-world apps for iOS and Android devices with 12 fantastic projects

1. Use PhoneGap 3.x effectively to build real, functional mobile apps ranging from productivity apps to a simple arcade game.

2. Explore often-used design patterns in apps designed for mobile devices.

3. Fully practical, project-based approach to give you the confidence in developing your app independently.

Please check **www.PacktPub.com** for information on our titles

Instant PhoneGap

ISBN: 9781782168690   Paperback: 64 pages

Begin your journey of building amazing mobile applications using PhoneGap with the geolocation API

1. Learn something new in an Instant! A short, fast, focused guide delivering immediate results.

2. Build your first app using the geolocation API, reading the XML file, and PhoneGap.

3. Full code provided along with illustrations, images, and cascading style sheets.

4. Develop an application in PhoneGap and submit it to app stores for different platforms.

PhoneGap Mobile Application Development Cookbook

ISBN: 9781849518581   Paperback: 320 pages

Over 40 recipes to create mobile applications using the PhoneGap API with examples and clear instructions

1. Use the PhoneGap API to create native mobile applications that work on a wide range of mobile devices.

2. Discover the native device features and functions you can access and include within your applications.

3. Packed with clear and concise examples to show you how to easily build native mobile applications.

Please check **www.PacktPub.com** for information on our titles